DOROTHEA LANGE
MIGRANT MOTHER

SARAH HERMANSON MEISTER

THE MUSEUM OF MODERN ART, NEW YORK

IT IS PERFECTLY LOGICAL TO WRITE ABOUT THE SINGULARITY OF A PAINTING, whereas photography's multiplicity is central to our understanding of the medium. The vast majority of photographs are made from negatives—or today, from digital files—from which it is possible, at least in theory, to make an infinite number of identical prints. The subject of this book, Dorothea Lange's *Migrant Mother*, exists in more formats, prints, and places than (arguably) any other photograph in the world. In this regard it is, ironically, singular.

Migrant Mother is also a singular icon of twentieth-century art. Lange made this photograph—along with six others of the same woman, Florence Owens Thompson, and her daughters—in Nipomo, California, in early March 1936. Since that time, the image has been so widely circulated that it is now a fixture in the public imagination. On March 10 Thompson's likeness appeared in tens of thousands of copies of the *San Francisco News*, and tens of thousands more with a follow-up article the next day. The impact of those photographs was quick and profound, not only on the community of migrant workers near Nipomo. One beleaguered federal employee wrote in July 1936: "We are snowed under with requests for migratory labor pictures. . . . All this material is being grasped at eagerly by all press services, newspapers, and magazines. We are getting the greatest spread that we have ever had."[1] In 1936 Lange was an employee of the United States government, so her images made during that period are in the public domain, which means that anyone could (and in fact still can) reproduce them for any purpose, free of charge. Surely this ease of access has contributed to the ubiquity of *Migrant Mother*. The U.S. Postal Service chose to use it on a thirty-two-cent stamp in 1998, adding millions of (slightly cropped) copies to its circulation history **[FIG. 1]**. It has appeared on dozens of book and magazine covers, has been transformed into a thousand-piece puzzle and a cross-stitch

Dorothea Lange (American, 1895–1965). *Migrant Mother, Nipomo, California*. 1936. Gelatin silver print, 11 ⅛ x 8 9/16" (28.3 x 21.8 cm). THE MUSEUM OF MODERN ART, NEW YORK. PURCHASE, 1949 (PROMOTED 1995)

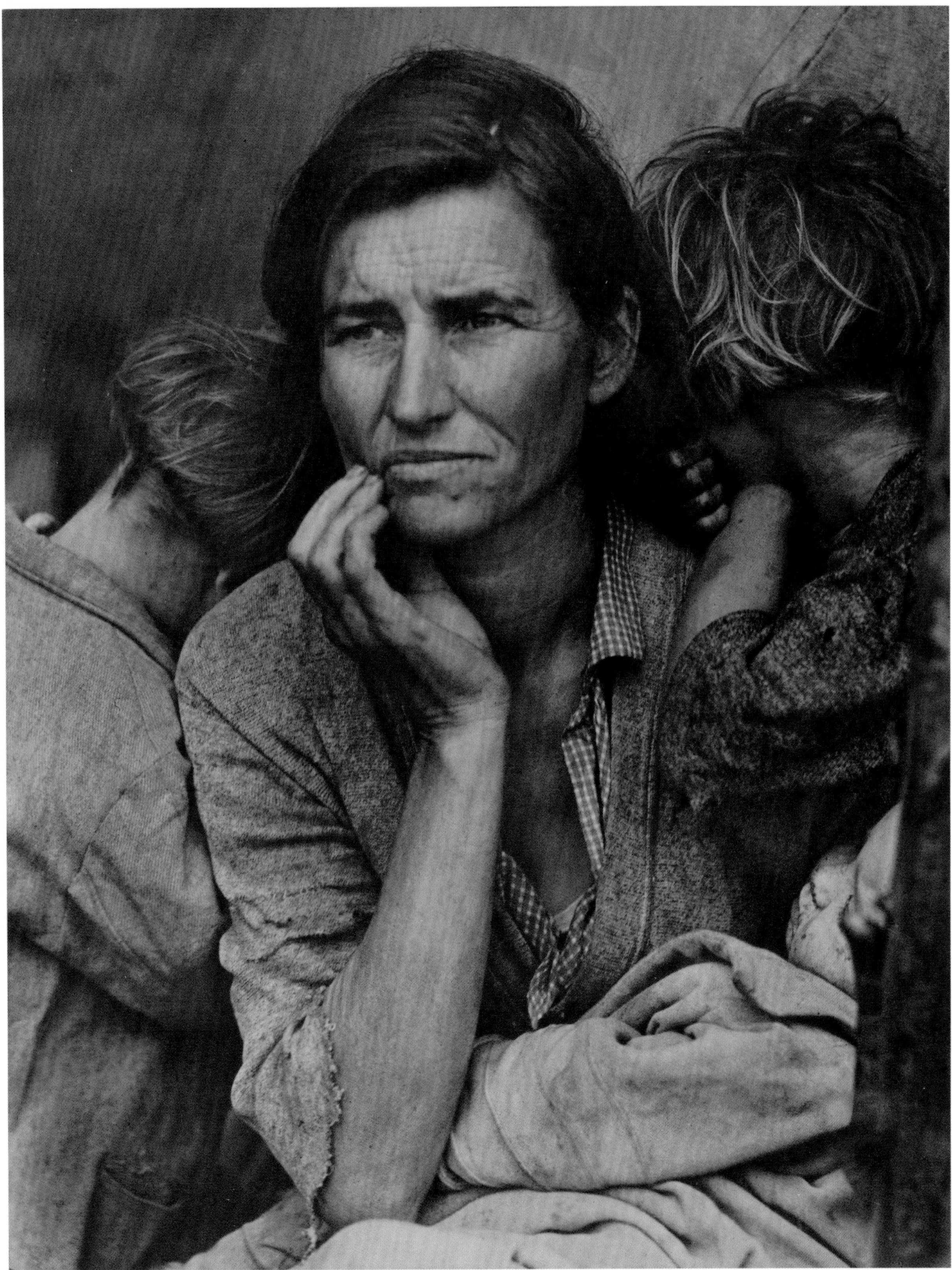

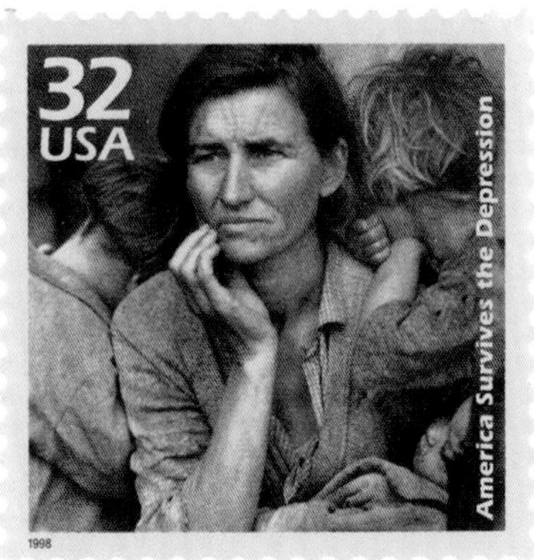

FIG. 1. Thirty-two-cent stamp issued by the U.S. Postal Service in 1998. PHOTOGRAPHY DEPARTMENTAL COLLECTION, THE MUSEUM OF MODERN ART, NEW YORK. PURCHASE, 2018

pattern, and has decorated countless trinkets and T-shirts, posters and postcards. Prints from Lange's negative have been included in landmark photography exhibitions seen by millions of people around the world, and shown in untold numbers of other displays, both public and private. The image has seeped into our common cultural consciousness. Even a scene from a 1967 Hollywood film carries with it echoes of Lange's photograph **[FIG. 2]**.[2] Its omnipresence—facilitated by the inherent reproducibility of the medium and encouraged by its powerful emotional impact—may be what most clearly distinguishes *Migrant Mother* from any other photograph.

—

Dorothea Nutzhorn was born on May 26, 1895, in Hoboken, New Jersey, the first child of two first-generation German Americans.[3] They lived comfortably, with ample access to music and literature. The family's only other child, Martin, was born in 1901. During the summer of 1902 Dorothea contracted polio, a potentially life-threatening virus that left her with permanent damage to her right leg and foot. As she later recalled: "I was physically disabled, and no one who hasn't lived the life of a semi-cripple knows how much that means. . . . [It] formed me, guided me, instructed me, helped me, and humiliated me. All those things at once."[4] The other defining trauma of her childhood occurred when she was twelve: her parents separated and (as she saw it) her father abandoned the family.

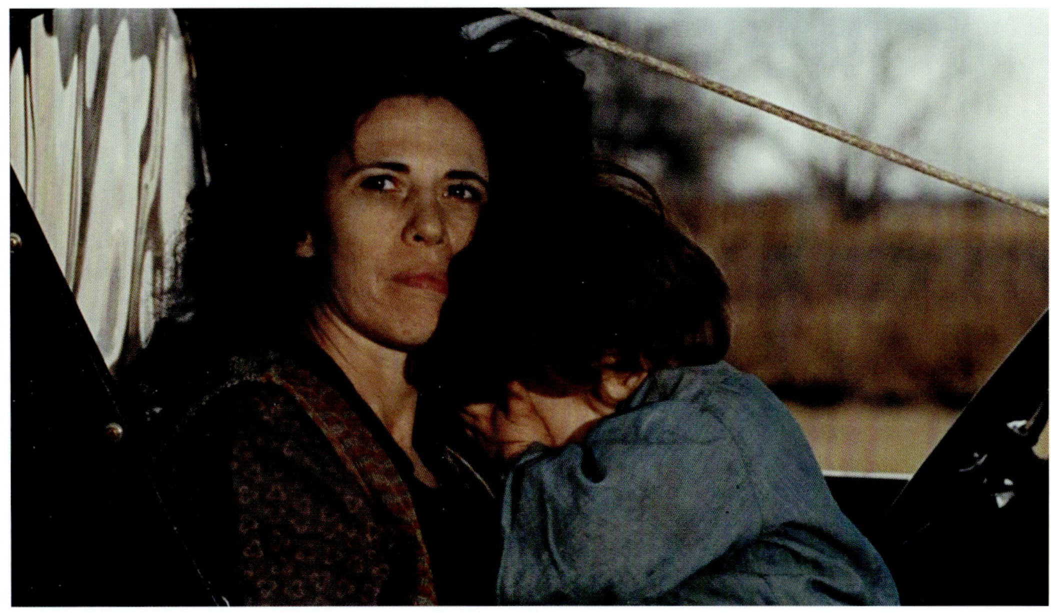

FIG. 2. Still from *Bonnie and Clyde*. 1967. Film: 35mm, color, sound, 111 minutes. Directed by Arthur Penn

Dorothea and her brother and mother moved in with her maternal grandmother in Hoboken. Her mother took a job at the Chatham Square Branch of the New York Public Library on the Lower East Side of Manhattan. Dorothea commuted into the city with her every day and began attending public school near the library. Later, she went to high school on Manhattan's Upper West Side and, upon graduation in 1912, declared her intention to become a photographer. Having never owned a camera, she first took a position in Arnold Genthe's studio (eventually she would apprentice with various other photographers) and augmented her practical training with a class taught by Clarence H. White at Columbia University's Teachers College. Both Genthe and White were adept at navigating the concerns of clients with their artistic ambitions; and their aesthetic approaches, while distinct, shared a pictorialist tendency toward soft-focus that would characterize Lange's early studio work.

In early 1918 Dorothea embarked upon what was intended to be a journey around the world with a high school classmate, Florence (Fronsie) Ahlstrom. By May they had reached San Francisco, where their savings were wiped out by a pickpocket. That misadventure closed the door on their travels, stranding them in the Bay Area, which would remain the photographer's home until her death in 1965. She took a job at Marsh & Company, a general goods store that sold, among other things, photographic supplies, and provided photo-finishing services. Perhaps sensing the significance of this liminal moment, the young job

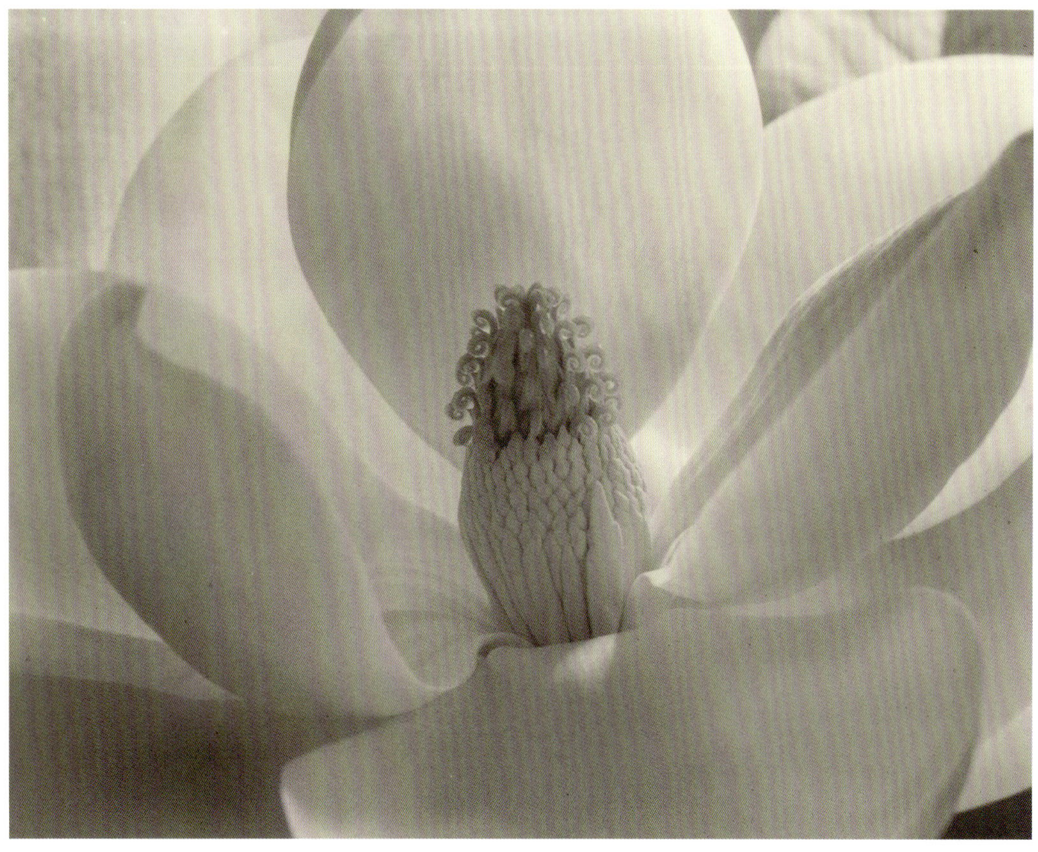

FIG. 3. Imogen Cunningham (American, 1883–1976). *Magnolia Blossom*. c. 1925. Gelatin silver print, 6 ¾ x 8 ½" (17.1 x 21.6 cm). THE MUSEUM OF MODERN ART, NEW YORK. GIFT OF ALBERT M. BENDER, 1939

seeker used her mother's maiden name, Lange, on the application, severing a final symbolic tie with her father.

Keen to connect with the photographic community, Lange soon joined the San Francisco Camera Club, and within a year, with money borrowed from friends, she opened her own photographic portrait studio at 540 Sutter Street. That studio became a gathering place for San Francisco's bohemian crowd, and it was there that she met the painter Maynard Dixon, whom she married in March 1920.[5] Photographer Imogen Cunningham was a close friend; her husband, Roi Partridge, had been one of Lange's first customers at Marsh & Company, and their son, Rondal, would later work as Lange's trusted assistant. Despite these close personal ties and their parallel studio-based practices, there were dramatic differences between Cunningham's and Lange's work. Cunningham embraced a rigorous clarity and delicate tonal range characteristic of contact prints from eight-by-ten-inch negatives **[FIG. 3]**, while Lange's first priority (at least through the early 1930s) was to

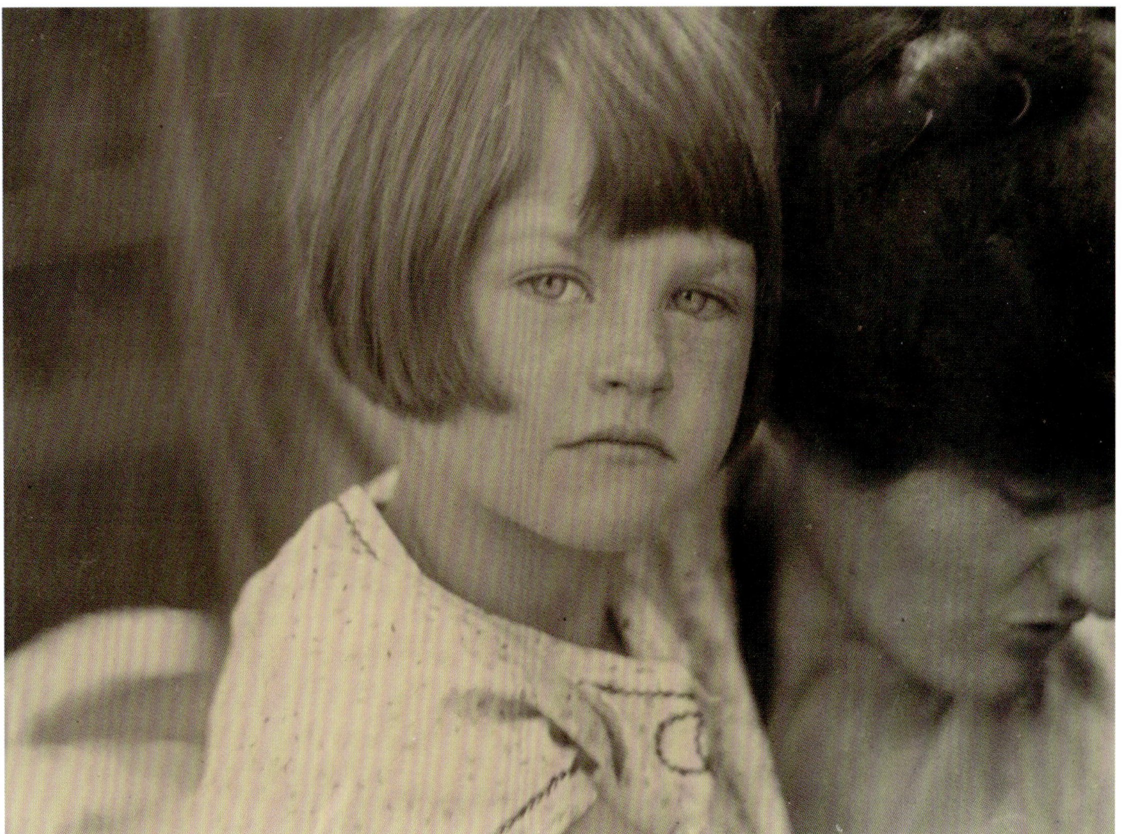

FIG. 4. Dorothea Lange (American, 1895–1965). *Clausen Child and Mother*. c. 1930. Gelatin silver print, 6 ⅛ x 8 ¼" (15.6 x 21 cm). THE MUSEUM OF MODERN ART, NEW YORK. THOMAS WALTHER COLLECTION. GIFT OF HENRI CARTIER-BRESSON, BY EXCHANGE, 2017

satisfy clients unlikely to relish such potentially unflattering detail, yet without adopting the fanciful tropes then common in studio practice. In her words:

> People like Imogen Cunningham, whom I knew very well by that time, all worked for name and prestige, and sent to exhibits. But I was a tradesman. At least so I regarded myself. And I was a professional photographer who had a product that was more honest, more truthful, and in some ways more charming. At any rate there was no false front in it. I really and seriously tried, with every person I photographed, to reveal them as closely as I could.[6]

Even within the bounds of traditional studio portraiture, Lange's images are notable for their ability to evoke a sense of relaxed intimacy, and for their unconventionally and artfully asymmetrical compositions [**FIG. 4**].

Lange and Dixon's first son, Daniel, arrived in May 1925, and their second, John, in June 1928; also in the home was Dixon's teenage daughter, Constance (Consie), from his first marriage. Although Lange maintained her studio, the competing demands of being a wife, mother, and professional photographer were compounded with the onset of the Great Depression in late 1929. Even their modest lifestyle was difficult to maintain, as demand for Lange's portraits and Dixon's paintings dwindled. After a short stint living in Taos, New Mexico, they moved back to San Francisco in 1932, and sent the boys to a school in Marin County, where they boarded with local families. Lange and Dixon gave up their shared home and moved into separate studios.

From her second-floor-studio window on Montgomery Street, Lange witnessed scenes of devastation wrought by the faltering economy. In early 1933, with trepidation and conviction in equal measure, she went down to photograph in the street for the first time. As she recalled: "I wasn't accustomed to jostling about in groups of tormented, depressed and angry men, with a camera."[7] One result was *White Angel Breadline*, an image that succinctly humanizes the impact of unemployment: a man grappling with poverty and hunger, alone in a sea of men in similarly dire straits **[FIG. 5]**. This photograph marked the beginning of a new chapter for Lange, who was becoming increasingly confident in her ability to use photography to confront the urgent circumstances around her. As the writer George P. Elliott would later note: "This image does not derive its power from formal elegance so much as from its being inextricably entangled with the comment it is making. It is art for life's sake."[8] The same may be said for much of Lange's work.

In 1934 Lange photographed the May Day demonstrations in San Francisco; shortly thereafter, the photographer Willard Van Dyke presented these images in his exhibition space in Oakland. Paul Taylor, a professor of agricultural economics at the University of California at Berkeley, describes his visit to the gallery and his first encounter with Lange's work:

> What fascinated me especially among her prints was one of a street agitator bellowing into a microphone at the San Francisco Civic Center. It fitted my current need exactly. In collaboration with a colleague at the university, I had just completed and sent to the *Survey Graphic* the draft of an article on San Francisco and the General Strike of 1934. I wanted that photograph to accompany it. The exhibitor, Willard Van Dyke, put me on the phone with Dorothea Lange; and her photograph became the frontispiece of our article. I think we paid her fifteen dollars for the photograph. That was money in those days.[9]

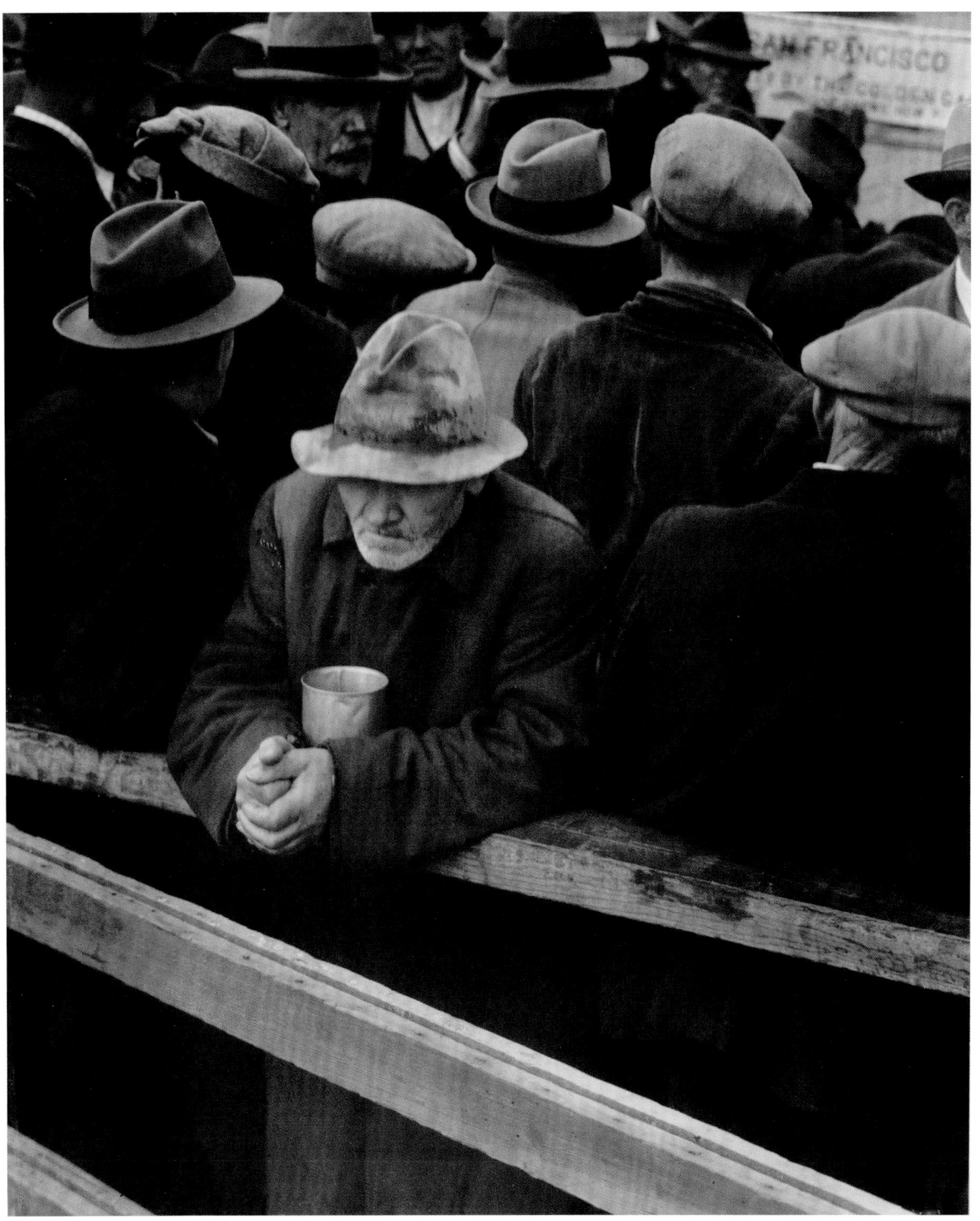

FIG. 5. Dorothea Lange (American, 1895–1965). *White Angel Breadline*. 1933. Gelatin silver print, 10 ¾ x 8 ⅞" (27.3 x 22.6 cm). THE MUSEUM OF MODERN ART, NEW YORK. GIFT OF ALBERT M. BENDER, 1940

In late 1934 Taylor was hired by the California State Emergency Relief Administration to study the contemporary circumstances of agriculture and migrant workers and recommend a program to help them. By early 1935 he had convinced his superiors to hire Lange as a typist—they had yet to be convinced of the need for a photographer—to accompany his team on research trips around California. In their first spiral-bound report, submitted on March 15, 1935, were fifty-seven photographs by Lange, including at least ten made in Nipomo and San Luis Obispo County, where she would create *Migrant Mother* the following year **[FIG. 6]**.[10] This was the first of many journeys Lange and Taylor would embark upon together, bound by a commitment to illuminate—and improve—the extraordinarily difficult circumstances around them. Taylor provided Lange with an intellectual framework for her natural sympathies; together, his scholarship and her keenly observed depictions became hugely influential in effecting public policy.[11] That summer, the state agency for which they both worked was transferred to the newly formed federal Resettlement Administration (RA; in 1937 renamed the Farm Security Administration, or FSA). Their personal mission was unchanged, although the official scope of their responsibilities was enlarged. By November they had divorced their respective spouses, and on December 6, 1935, they interrupted their work only long enough to be married by a justice of the peace in Albuquerque, New Mexico.

—

In 1934 Van Dyke noted: "Miss Lange's real interest is in human beings and her urge to photograph is aroused only when human values are concerned." He went on to clarify: "Unlike the newspaper reporter, she has no news or editorial policies to direct her movements; it is only her deeply personal sympathies for the unfortunates, the downtrodden, the misfits, among her contemporaries that provide the impetus for her expedition."[12] Time and again, this observation would be confirmed, most memorably in the photograph that would come to be known as *Migrant Mother.* Lange's evident compassion for a destitute thirty-two-year-old mother of seven children is an essential element inspiring the powerful response to this now-iconic photograph. The fact that Lange was an

FIG. 6. Dorothea Lange (American, 1895–1965). "Camp of white American pea pickers. Nipomo, Calif. / Mexican pea pickers' camp. Nipomo. / Jan. 26, 1935," in Paul S. Taylor, *Establishment of Rural Rehabilitation Camps for Migrants in California*, report of March 15, 1935. FARM SECURITY ADMINISTRATION–OFFICE OF WAR INFORMATION PHOTOGRAPH COLLECTION, LIBRARY OF CONGRESS

Note: The image captions in quotation marks are taken verbatim from the Resettlement Administration/Farm Security Administration files, now with the Library of Congress. They were often drawn from Lange's notes. Those for the Migrant Mother series were likely derived (by Lange or an RA/FSA staff member) from United Press reports published in the San Francisco News *and elsewhere in March 1936. The Library of Congress reference numbers for individual Lange negatives appear on page 47 of this volume.*

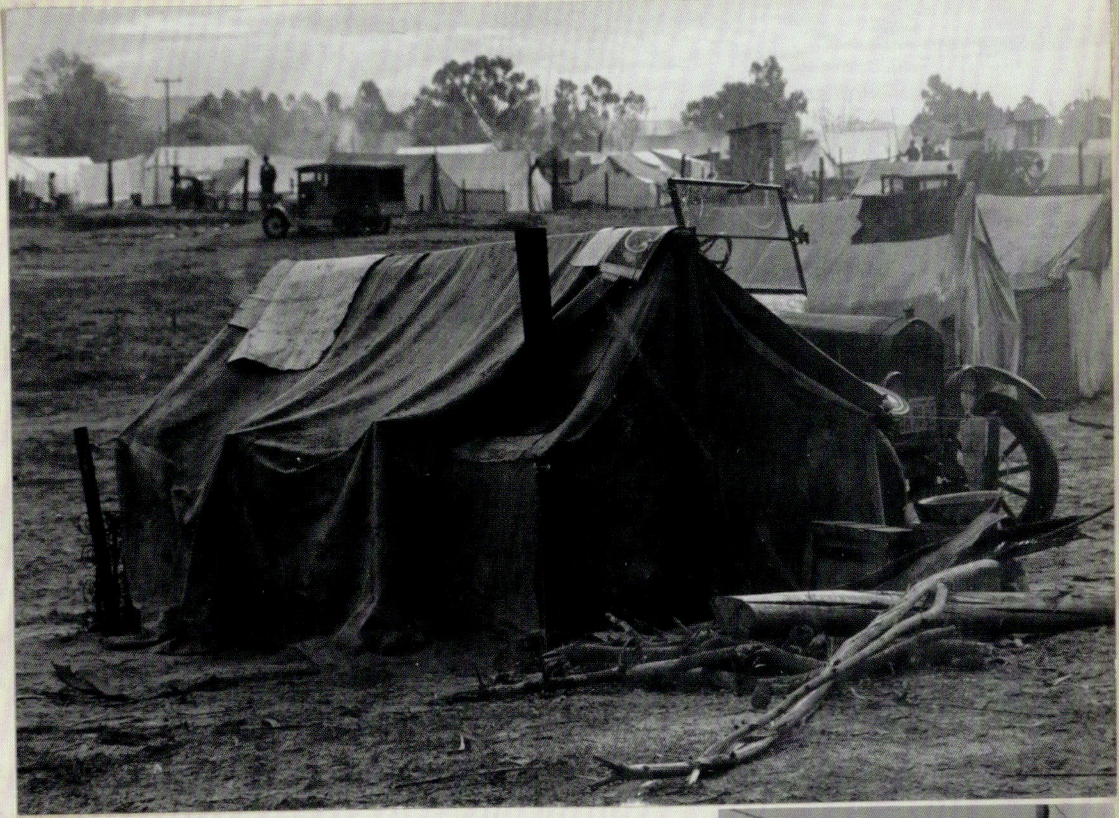

Camp of white American pea pickers.
Nipomo, Calif.

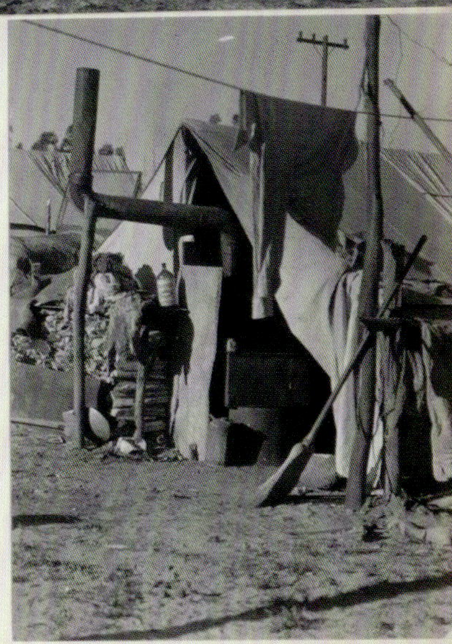

Mexican pea pickers'
camp.
Nipomo -

Jan 26 - 1935

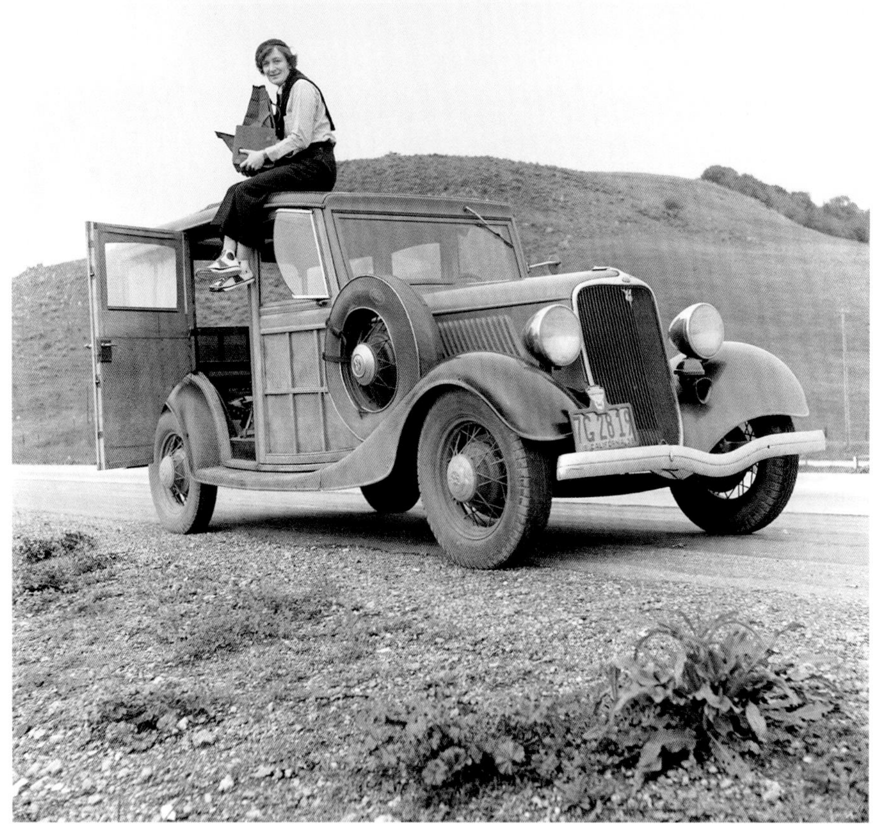

FIG. 7. "Dorothea Lange on the Job." February 1936. FARM SECURITY ADMINISTRATION–OFFICE OF WAR INFORMATION PHOTOGRAPH COLLECTION, LIBRARY OF CONGRESS

employee of the federal government—as she was, with a few interruptions, from mid-1935 through late 1939—had no impact on the character of her work, although it helped pay the bills and dramatically expanded her audience **[FIG. 7]**. In the days before databases, thumbing through the FSA files in Washington, D.C., was the most efficient way to access her works from this period, as countless researchers did: the worn corners of the file card to which an early reference print of *Migrant Mother* was affixed testify to the enduring interest in this image **[FIG. 8]**.[13]

By March 1936 Lange had been by herself on the road in California for several weeks and was understandably eager to get home.[14] She recalls initially driving past the sign for a pea-pickers camp, but then—twenty miles on—feeling inexplicably compelled to turn back. When she arrived at the camp she exposed a handful of negatives. Unusually for Lange, she spoke only briefly to the woman before her camera.[15] Slightly less unusual was the fact that Lange did not note her name: Florence Owens Thompson.[16] The sequence of these seven images

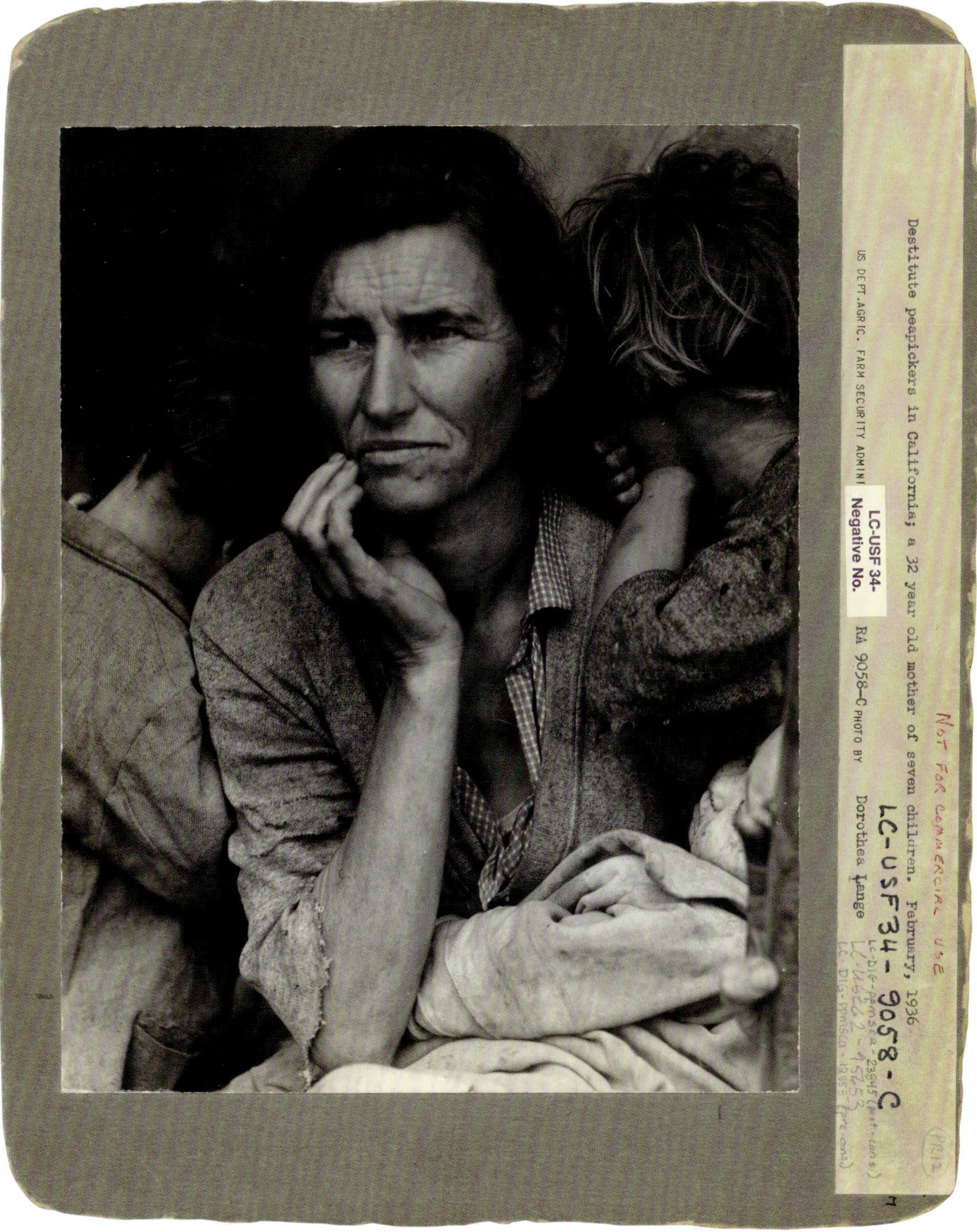

FIG. 8. Dorothea Lange (American, 1895–1965). "Destitute peapickers in California; a 32 year old mother of seven children. February [*sic*: March] 1936." Gelatin silver print mounted on board, image: 9 ⅛ x 7 1⁄16" (23.1 x 18 cm). FARM SECURITY ADMINISTRATION–OFFICE OF WAR INFORMATION PHOTOGRAPH COLLECTION, LIBRARY OF CONGRESS

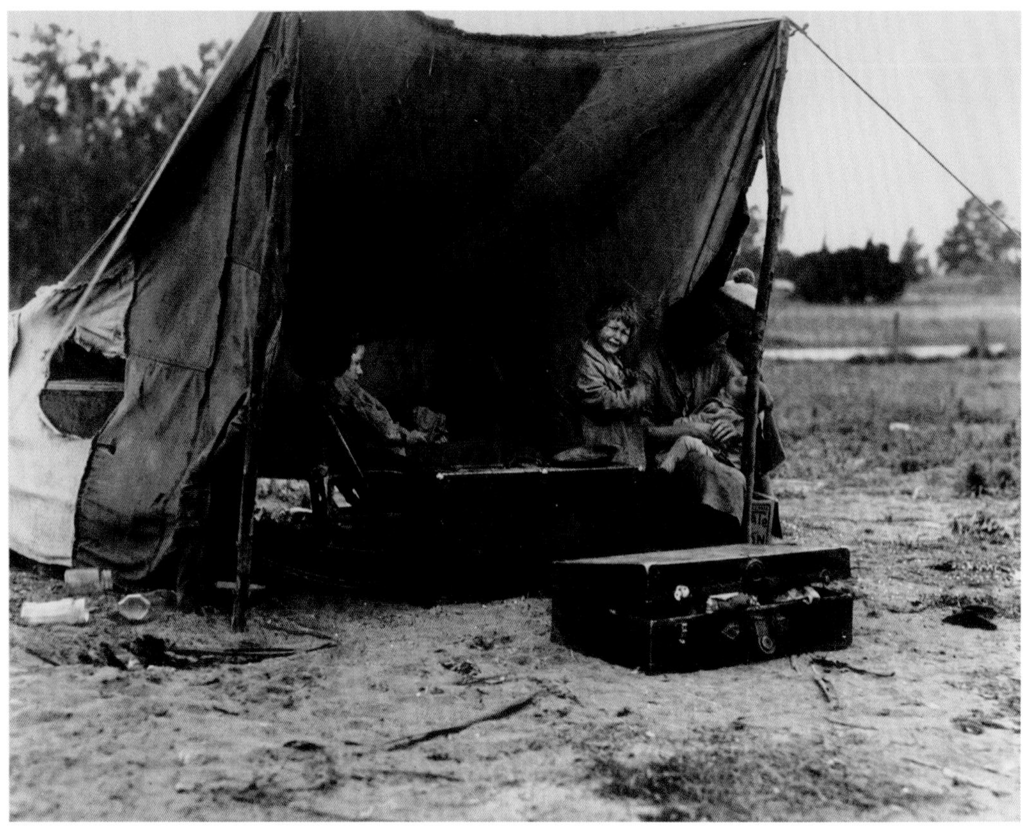

FIG. 9. Dorothea Lange (American, 1895–1965). From the Migrant Mother series. March 1936. Gelatin silver print, 7 11⁄16 x 9 9⁄16" (19.5 x 24.3 cm). COURTESY THE DOROTHEA LANGE COLLECTION, OAKLAND MUSEUM OF CALIFORNIA, CITY OF OAKLAND. GIFT OF PAUL S. TAYLOR

cannot be determined with certainty, but Lange remembers moving "closer and closer."[17] In one of two frames taken from a slight distance, in which the full lean-to tent is visible, only one child seems to be aware of Lange's presence. This picture was not included with the group of five Lange chose to send to the RA in Washington, D.C., presumably because she believed it was less successful **[FIG. 9]**. In the other image made from approximately this distance, the figures are more deliberately arranged: Thompson's twelve-year-old daughter, Viola, faces Lange; she is perched in a rocking chair, now in front of the tent in which her mother and siblings take shelter **[FIG. 10]**.[18] Everyone in this image (except the baby) is looking directly at Lange, yet she was likely unsatisfied with the imbalance of the exposure: other than Viola, they all appear in the tent's shadow.[19]

Moving a bit closer, Lange exposed four more four-by-five-inch negatives. One of these features Thompson nursing the youngest child, Norma, then not quite a year old **[FIG. 11]**; another shows Thompson, still nursing the baby, with

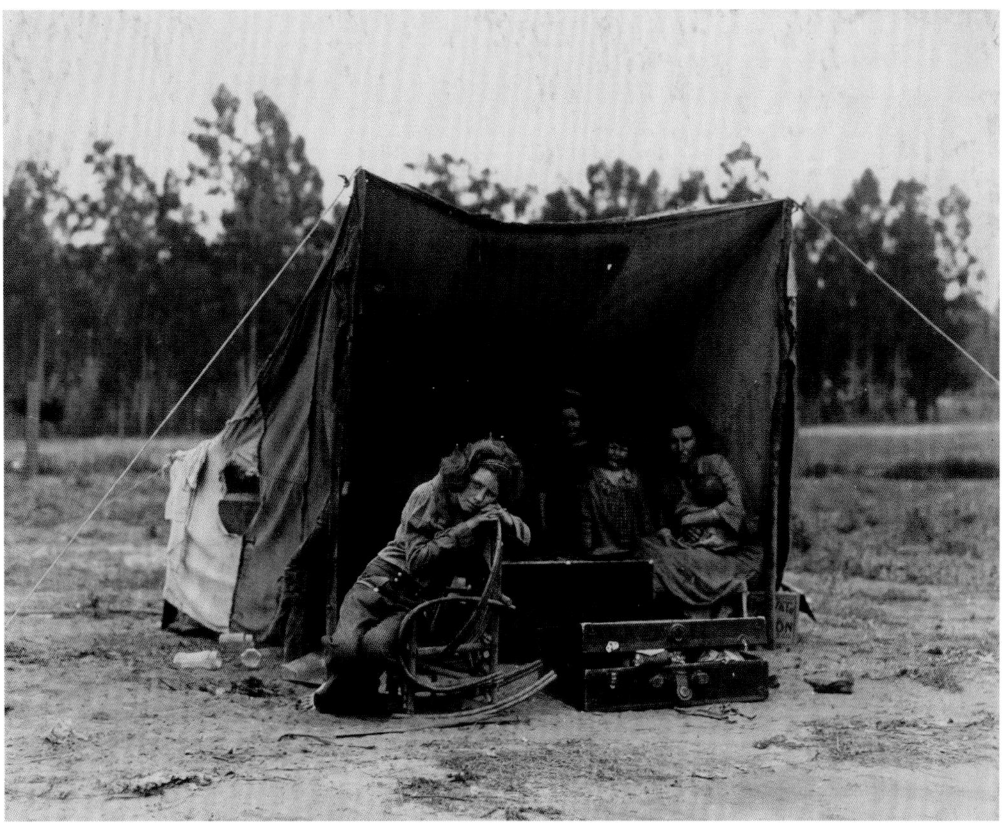

FIG. 10. Dorothea Lange (American, 1895–1965). "Nipomo, Calif. March 1936. Migrant agricultural worker's family. Seven hungry children and their mother, aged 32. The father is a native Californian." Gelatin silver print, 7 3/8 x 9 5/16" (18.8 x 23.6 cm). FARM SECURITY ADMINISTRATION–OFFICE OF WAR INFORMATION PHOTOGRAPH COLLECTION, LIBRARY OF CONGRESS

the next youngest, Katherine, squinting quizzically—a little-known image likely set aside by Lange **[FIG. 12]**. The remaining two pictures made from this distance show six-year-old Ruby (now with her hat removed) leaning on Thompson's left shoulder. In neither of these do the subjects look directly at the camera; their averted gazes may have struck Lange as promising: she captured this arrangement as both a vertical and a horizontal image **[FIGS. 13, 14]**.[20]

Lange moved even closer and exposed the negative of Thompson with her three youngest children. With that, she had created an image that would become an icon, symbolizing the Depression and the dire straits of agricultural workers—a photograph that would (to Lange's occasional chagrin) overshadow all others in her long and distinguished career. Her taut composition excludes all but the most essential information. In lieu of the girls' faces, we see their tousled heads nestling against their mother's shoulders; their anonymity serves to lend these familial bonds a sense of universality. Still, Lange's large negative captures a wealth

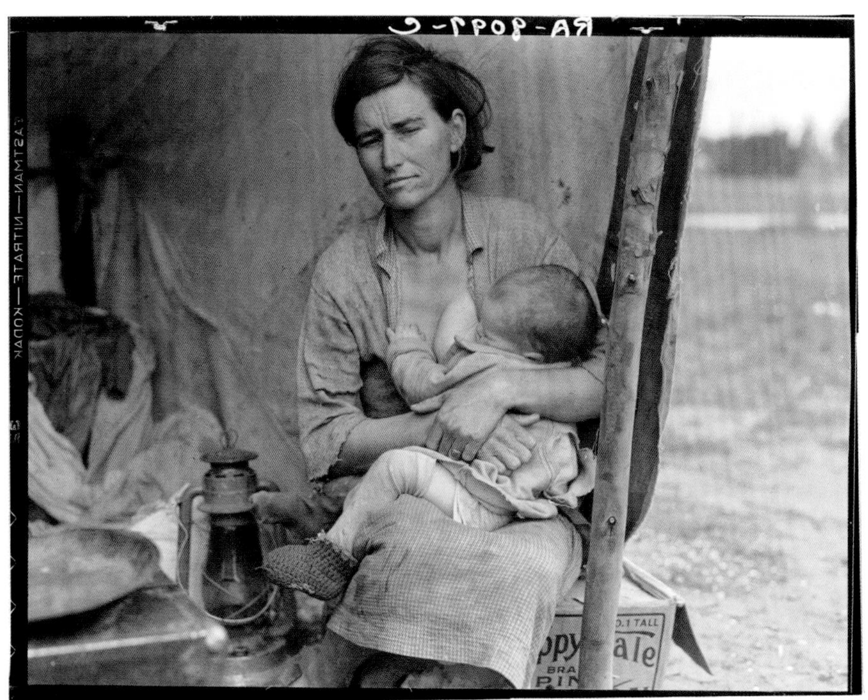

FIG. 11. Dorothea Lange (American, 1895–1965). “Nipomo, Calif. Mar. 1936. Migrant agricultural worker’s family. Seven hungry children. Mother aged 32. Father is native Californian.” Digital file from 4 x 5" (10.2 x 12.7 cm) negative. FARM SECURITY ADMINISTRATION–OFFICE OF WAR INFORMATION PHOTOGRAPH COLLECTION, LIBRARY OF CONGRESS

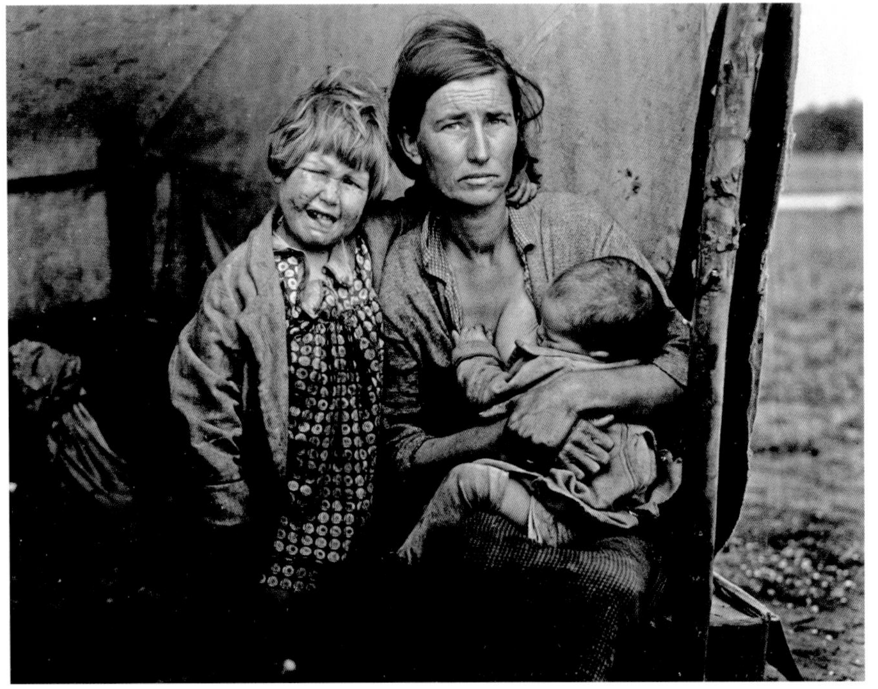

FIG. 12. Dorothea Lange (American, 1895–1965). From the Migrant Mother series. March 1936. Gelatin silver print, 5 x 4" (12.7 x 10.2 cm). COURTESY THE DOROTHEA LANGE COLLECTION, OAKLAND MUSEUM OF CALIFORNIA, CITY OF OAKLAND. GIFT OF PAUL S. TAYLOR

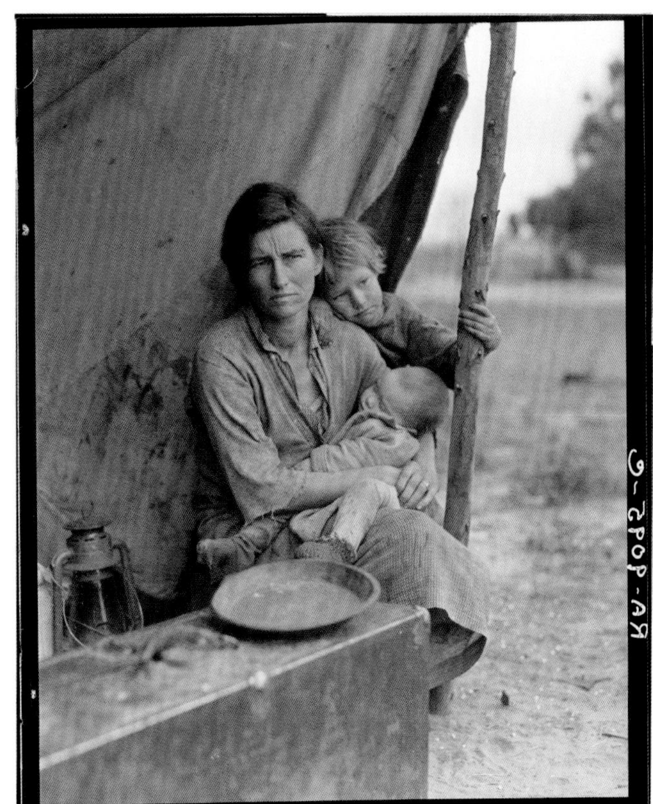

FIG. 13. Dorothea Lange (American, 1895–1965). "Migrant agricultural worker's family. Seven children without food. Mother aged 32, father is a native Californian. March 1936." Digital file from 4 x 5" (10.2 x 12.7 cm) negative. FARM SECURITY ADMINISTRATION–OFFICE OF WAR INFORMATION PHOTOGRAPH COLLECTION, LIBRARY OF CONGRESS

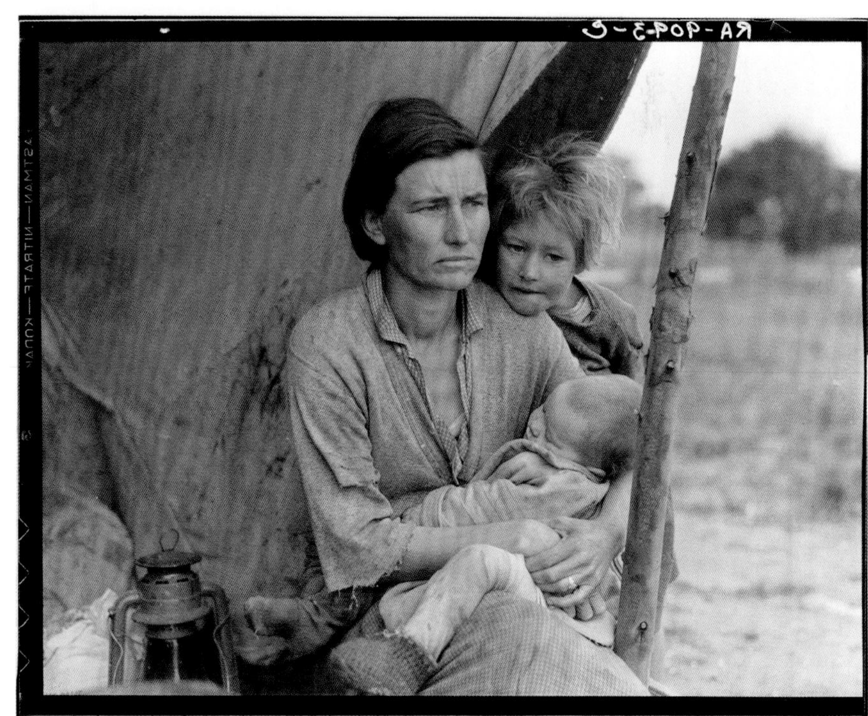

FIG. 14. Dorothea Lange (American, 1895–1965). "Nipomo, Calif. Mar. 1936. Migrant agricultural worker's family. Seven hungry children. Mother aged 32, the father is a native Californian. Destitute in pea pickers camp, because of the failure of the early pea crop. These people had just sold their tent in order to buy food. Most of the 2500 people in this camp were destitute." Digital file from 4 x 5" (10.2 x 12.7 cm) negative. FARM SECURITY ADMINISTRATION–OFFICE OF WAR INFORMATION PHOTOGRAPH COLLECTION, LIBRARY OF CONGRESS

of detail that anchors our experience in specific fact: from the frayed fabric to Thompson's weary, concerned, strikingly beautiful face. It is, rightfully, the most memorable and most widely reproduced of the series. The superlatives that have been heaped upon it have done nothing to dilute its impact, nor have the passing decades diminished our inclination to empathize with the subjects' plight.

The effects of Lange's visit on the lives of the migrant community came quickly. On March 9, 1936, the front page of the *San Francisco News* featured the headline "2500 Rescued from Hunger by SRA Action," and Lange, though not mentioned by name, is credited as a Resettlement Administration photographer who "accidentally" discovered "the desperate plight of the ragged, starving colony" **[FIG. 15]**. The following day, two photographs from her sequence accompanied a United Press wire article titled "Food Rushed to Starving Farm Colony," and the *San Francisco News* also printed an impassioned editorial encouraging better cooperation between the state and the Resettlement Administration **[FIG. 16]**.

The San Francisco News, Monday, March 9, 1936

2500 RESCUED FROM HUNGER BY SRA ACTION

Starving Community Found Accidentally 35 Miles South of San Luis Obispo / FARM WORKERS STRANDED / Failure of Pea Crop Responsible for Plight; Food Is Rushed

On the outskirts of the little town of Nipomo, 35 miles south of San Luis Obispo, 2500 persons, the majority of them children, were saved from starvation today.

Foodstuffs were rushed to them by the Surplus Commodities Division of SRA [State Relief Administration] as red tape was cut to alleviate further suffering.

The remnant of California's army of migratory agricultural workers, they had come to Nipomo weeks ago to pick peas, were stranded when protracted rains destroyed the crop.

Found Accidentally

Many of them had been lured from their homes, they said, by advertisements of work in the pea fields, according to reports here.

The desperate plight of the ragged, starving colony was discovered accidentally by a photographer for the Resettlement Administration, who forwarded the report to W. B. Jenkins, state director of the Surplus Commodities Division.

He immediately ordered a survey by E. M. Brown, Los Angeles, assistant state director, resulting in the dispatching of food. It is expected the Government will be forced to take care of the workers and their families until the next pea crop, which will not be for a month or six weeks.

This is the story investigators brought back to Federal relief authorities here:

Huddled in their open camp just outside Nipomo, the colony lived through weeks of almost constant rain as they awaited work. Many were without shelter of any kind; others, more fortunate, lived in leaky tents, hastily constructed rude huts or slept in their battered automobiles.

When word came the crop had been destroyed and there would be no work until late April or May, two-thirds of the workers had enough left to get out, but 2500 were left behind.

Sickness Stalks Camp

To keep themselves in food, they had sold their clothing, blankets, parts of their autos, anything of value. Families pooled their resources, took care of each other as best they could. Meanwhile, children and adults, emaciated by hunger, became ill with colds and sickness swept the camp.

The colony appealed to Nipomo authorities for help, asked the various relief agencies, but as they did not come under any of the various categories, assistance was denied them.

Only the timely arrival of the Resettlement Administration photographer, who had visited the camp before the exodus of the first group and returned to find the stranded workers in a much more desperate condition, saved them from starvation.

Tents Sold for Food

In past years, the pea crop at San Luis Obispo has been picked chiefly by Mexicans, but this year Americans, most of them with large families, sought the work.

They pitched camp on a site where the Mexicans had lived before them. It was sanitary and there was plenty of water, but there was no shelter.

In destitute circumstances, many of the workers arrived almost empty-handed, expecting to find immediate work. Others who had tents were forced to sell them for food.

Part of the food which will be sent to Nipomo will be purchased from a self-help co-operative cannery at Astascadero, Winslow Carleton, state director of the self-help co-operative service, revealed. The money the cannery receives will be used to retire the last of a $5000 grant they obtained from the state to start the project.

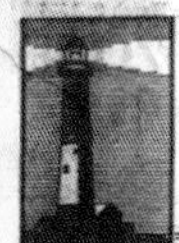

The San Francisco News

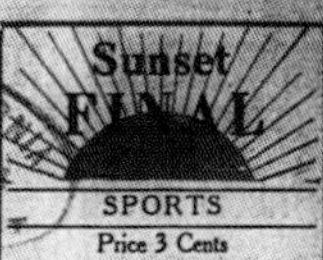

Local Forecast: Warmer tonight and tomorrow with gentle to moderate northerly winds. (Complete report on Page 11.)

Vol. 34 Entered as second class matter, San Francisco, Calif., postoffice. SAN FRA[NCISCO], MONDAY, MARCH 9, 1936 D Sold by newsstands and on trains, 5 cents per copy. No. 59

HITLER PEACE PLAN SPURNED

'Recall Troops First,' Say France and Belgium

2500 RESCUED FROM HUNGER BY SRA ACTION

Starving Community Found Accidentally 35 Miles South of San Luis Obispo

FARM WORKERS STRANDED

Failure of Pea Crop Responsible for Plight; Food Is Rushed

On the outskirts of the little town of Nipomo, 35 miles south of San Luis Obispo, 2500 persons, the majority of them children, were saved from starvation today.

Foodstuffs were rushed to them by the Surplus Commodities Division of SRA as red tape was cut to alleviate further suffering.

The remnant of California's army of migratory agricultural workers, they had come to Nipomo weeks ago to pick peas, were stranded when protracted rains destroyed the crop.

Found Accidentally

Many of them had been lured from their homes, they said, by advertisements of work in the pea fields, according to reports here.

The desperate plight of the ragged, starving colony was discovered accidentally by a photographer for the Resettlement Administration, who forwarded the report to W. B. Jenkins, state director of the Surplus Commodities Division.

He immediately ordered a survey by E. M. Brown, Los Angeles, assistant state director, resulting in the dispatching of food. It is expected the Government will be forced to take care of the workers and their families until the next pea crop, which will not be for a month or six weeks.

This is the story investigators brought back to Federal relief authorities here:

Huddled in their open camp just outside Nipomo, the colony lived through weeks of almost constant rain as they awaited work. Many were without shelter of any kind; others, more fortunate, lived in leaky tents, hastily constructed rude huts or slept in their battered automobiles.

When word came the crop had been destroyed and there would be no work until late April or May, two-thirds of the workers had enough left to get out, but 2500 were left behind.

Sickness Stalks Camp

To keep themselves in food, they had sold their clothing, blankets, parts of their autos, anything of value. Families pooled their resources, took care of each other as best they could. Meanwhile, children and adults, emaciated by hun-

(Turn to Page 3, Column 1)

JOCKEY IS SET DOWN

Florida Board Grounds Don Meade for Life for Bet Violation

By United Press

MIAMI, Fla., March 9.—The Florida State Racing Commission today revoked the jockey license of Don Meade with the indication he was put on the ground for life.

A brief statement by Walter H. Donovan, commission secretary, said Meade had been found guilty of violation of the rules governing betting by jockeys.

FIRST PICTURES OF TOKIO REBELLION

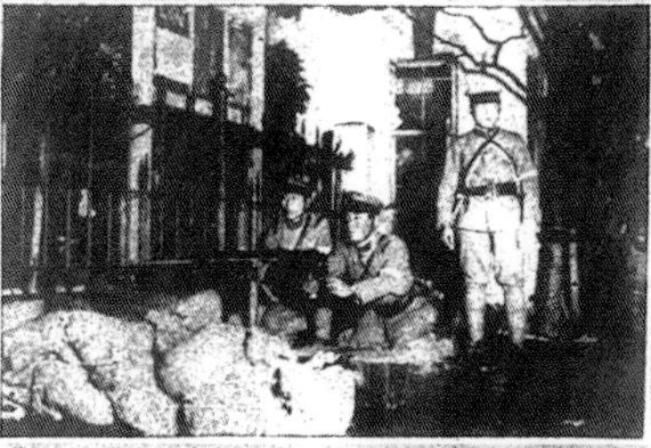

These pictures were taken when rebellion flared in Tokio, resulting in murder of leading statesmen, the formation of a new cabinet (see Page A), and the suicide of several leaders of the outbreak. The picture above shows a machine gun detachment of loyal soldiers near Hibiya Public Hall.

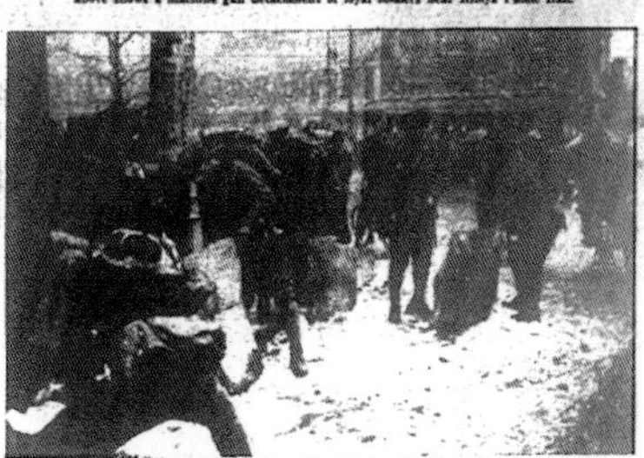

Loyal soldiers fill bags with snow to make a barricade.

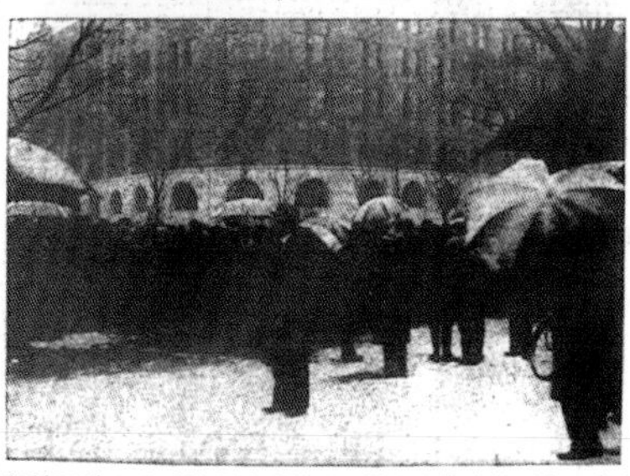

Spectators on the morning of Feb. 26 in front of the Home Ministry Building looking at the squads of soldiers on guard. These pictures arrived for The News on the China Clipper.

IL DUCE SENDS PARIS OFFER OF FRIENDSHIP

League's Peace Proposal for Africa Is Tentatively Accepted

BUT WAR WILL CONTINUE

Chamber of Deputies Meets in Rome, Votes Huge Military Fund

By United Press

ROME, March 9.—Italy has promised France to help force Germany to respect the Locarno Treaty, high authorities said today. Significantly the Chamber of Deputies met to vote the largest military appropriation since the World War.

And Italy, having promised France her support against Germany's treaty violations, proclaimed again her intention of continuing the Ethiopian war to a successful conclusion.

Italy has tentatively accepted the proposal of the League of Nations to listen to peace talks and there is a lull in military operations in Africa.

Nevertheless, when the Chamber of Deputies convened today in the presence of Premier Benito Musso-

WOULD TALK PEACE

By United Press

GENEVA, March 9.—The Ethiopian minister in Paris, Wolde Mariam, this afternoon sent a note to the secretariat of the League of Nations expressing Ethiopia's willingness to negotiate "a just and lasting peace" with Italy.

lini and all members of the government, Costanzo Ciano, press minister, assured the applauding deputies the war has not been abandoned.

The Italian pledge to France was communicated secretly. Its nature was revealed only unofficially, but from sources always close to Fascist policy. It was happily timed to evoke a kindly regard in Paris for Italian friendship, a few hours before Premier Benito Mussolini answers the League of Nations proposals for peace in Ethiopia.

Paraphrased, according to informants, the Italian communication to France said that Italy's regard for Italo-French friendship had been in no way altered by French indecision in the Ethiopian crisis. Italy considers such friendship "indispensable to the peace of Europe," the message reportedly said.

© 1936, United Press

2 MOTORBIKE RIDERS COLLIDE; 1 KILLED

Fatal Crash Occurs at Livermore Picnic Grounds

A collision between two motorcycles at the entrance to a Livermore picnic grounds killed one of the riders yesterday. He was Waner Nichols, 22, Oakland. Frank Pilot, 20, Oakland, riding the other machine, suffered a possible skull fracture.

Both were attending an outing of the Oakland Motorcycle Club.

Solid Front Presented By Former War Allies

By United Press

PARIS, March 9.—Belgium agreed fully with France tonight that Germany's troops must be withdrawn from the Rhineland before any negotiations on Adolf Hitler's suggestions for a European agreement can be considered.

Conversations between Premier Paul Van Zeeland of Belgium and Premier Albert Sarraut and Foreign Minister Pierre-Etienne Flandin of France showed the two countries to be in complete agreement on the subject.

Other developments:

Britain promised military aid to France and Belgium if they are attacked by Germany, but also agreed to consider Hitler's proposal for new treaties. France received official assurance of support in any crisis from Italy, Poland, the Little Entente, the Balkan Entente.

The Little Entente comprises Romania, Czecho-Slovakia and Jugo-Slavia. Jugo-Slavia, Greece and Turkey are in the Balkan Entente.

French frontier forces were greatly strengthened and Premier Sarraut said, "We are prepared to go to the very end" to resist German occupancy of the Rhineland. Paris was disappointed at Britain's conciliatory attitude. (Details on Page B.)

Germany followed up its violation of the treaty clauses forbidding militarization of the Rhineland by incorporating all state police in the Rhineland into the army, and declaring her rivers again entirely German and not international waterways, as provided by the treaty.

German troops continued to pour into the area and it was estimated 45,000 in all were there.

It was indicated officially Germany would refuse an invitation to attend Friday's meeting of the League Council on the crisis, taking the ground that legally she must be invited formally after the Council is in session.

SUDDEN OUTBREAK ON BORDER FEARED AS TROOPS MOBILIZE

U. S. Experts Declare Early Clash Unlikely So Long as Orders of European Officials Are Strictly Obeyed on Frontiers

By United Press

WASHINGTON, March 9.—No one here today says bloodshed is impossible as a result of Nazi troops' occupation of the Rhineland. But the opinion is widely held that an immediate clash is improbable.

The possibility most feared is an outburst of violence—an attack by French citizens on Nazi troopers or vice versa. Tempers are hot. So are words, official and otherwise. Britain alone, apparently, is maintaining its emotional equilibrium.

Desperate Gesture

Hitler's spectacular action is interpreted here primarily as a final desperate gesture to block ratification of the Franco-Soviet mutual assistance pact. It is so regarded on the continent.

The occupation has been in the cards a long time. It is part of the inevitable disintegration of the Versailles Treaty. That Germany would eventually reclaim the Rhineland was taken for granted.

The Franco-Soviet Treaty merely served as Hitler's wedge. By construing it to mean violation of the Locarno pact of 1925, he was able to repudiate the war boundaries fixed in that document, which was guaranteed by Britain, Italy and Belgium.

The Nazi dictator sees the Franco-Soviet pact putting strong armies at his front and back doors, each pledged to help the other should the Reich leader throw his ever-increasing legions into the field.

Safety Valve

That the occupation will inspire heated debates in half a dozen Parliaments, and many diplomatic meetings, secret and otherwise, may be assumed, but such events are regarded here hopefully as the safety valve which will prevent war if it can be prevented.

The Rhineland for years has been a political irritant like Alsace-Lorraine. Depriving Germany of this territory was opposed after the war by Lloyd George and President Wilson, who believed such a course would create another Alsace and thus another war.

Subsequent occupation of the Ruhr under the stolid, unyielding Poincare, when reparations did not come fast enough or not at all, piled up more fuel of dissent which flamed dangerously as Poincare finally quartered Negro colonial troops in the Rhineland towns. This aroused vigorous protests in England.

Setback From U. S.

There followed the hysteria of inflation with its economic wreckage in the Reich. Britain refused to cooperate with France in enforcing reparations. The former Allies were no longer unanimous in upholding the Versailles Treaty and that document suffered another major setback, the first having been the refusal of the United States Senate to ratify it.

The Locarno pact was then projected into a dangerously aroused Europe. After considerable sacrifices by Britain, France and Germany the status quo of Western Europe was fixed. It was after this meeting that Briand said:

"At Locarno we spoke European, a new language which we ought certainly to learn."

The Dawes Plan

This brought Germany into the League. Then came the Dawes and Young plans and partial evacuation of the Rhineland by France. Things appeared on the surface to be assuming a bit more stability.

Presently, however, occurred the reparations breakdown at Lausanne, failure of the disarmament conference, the ascent of Hitler and the Anglo-German naval agreement. The Versailles Treaty was becoming more and more a shadow of its former self.

Today, even the shadow becomes more vague with Nazi troops in the Rhineland.

EDEN PLEDGES AID AGAINST NAZI ATTACK

Baldwin Also Addresses House, Urges Huge Rearmament Program

NEXT STEP UP TO GENEVA

London Will Take No Further Action Until After Friday Meeting

By United Press

LONDON, March 9.—Britain will go to the military aid of France and Belgium if Germany attacks either while the situation caused by her rearming of the Rhineland is under consideration, Capt. Anthony Eden, foreign secretary, announced in the House of Commons today.

Capt. Eden stated the British Government's position to a crowded House, which included Norman H. Davis of the United States and the ambassadors of the leading powers in the galleries.

Prime Minister Stanley Baldwin also addressed the House, urging support of the government's huge rearmament program and warning aggressor nations that if Britain is attacked, she will be ready for them.

Capt. Eden explained the League of Nations must handle the situation and until the Council meets on Friday, no decision on what to do can be made.

'No Hostilities Implied'

However, "There is no reason to suppose that the German action implies a threat of hostilities," Capt. Eden assured the House.

Capt. Eden said that only last Friday he had suggested to the German ambassador a discussion of an air defense pact in Western Europe, but that "the German Government's course has profoundly shaken confidence in any engagement into which the Government of Germany might in future enter."

Nevertheless, he declared, Great Britain will consider the proposals for a new European peace agreement which Fuehrer Adolf Hitler advanced in his speech to the Reichstag Saturday. They included a 25-year peace agreement with France and Belgium.

"His Majesty's Government," Capt. Eden said, "will examine the new German proposals clear-sightedly and objectively, with a view to finding out the extent to which they represent means by which the shaken structure of peace again may be strengthened.

To Defend Allies

"His Majesty's Government," Capt. Eden continued, "think it necessary to say that should there take place, during the period which will be necessary for the consideration of the new situation, any actual attack on France or Belgium which would constitute a violation of Article 2 of the Locarno Treaty, His Majesty's Government, notwithstanding the German repudiation of the treaty, would regard themselves as honor bound to come in the manner provided by the treaty to the assistance of the country attacked."

In face of the crisis, Capt. Eden appealed to all sections of opinion to support the government.

"I feel justified in asking all sections of opinion in the House for

(Turn to Page 8 Column 8)

DOUG, BRIDE IN SPAIN

BARCELONA, Spain, March 9.—Douglas Fairbanks and his bride, the former Lady Ashley, arrived by airplane today.

LAST MINUTE NEWS

WRITES BONUS NOTE, THEN KILLS SELF

LOS ANGELES, March 9.—Ernest E. Mitchell, 45, former prosperous engraver, wrote a note of instruction today as to how his soldier's bonus should be spent, then killed himself by swallowing poison, according to police. The note requested that police notify his brother, Gordon Mitchell of San Jose.

INSIDE THE NEWS

NUDIE ON 'GOODWILL' TOUR

SAN DIEGO, March 9. — Tanya Cubitt, fully clothed, stepped aboard a United Air Lines plane today bound for New York on a "nudist goodwill tour" she hopes will land her the queenship of the Exposition nature-lovers.

RACE NEWS PAGE 14

CLIPPER HOME AGAIN

Carrying a pound of sugar for Vice-President John N. Garner and 200 pounds of airmail and other express, Pan-American Airways' China Clipper landed at Alameda at 2:05 p. m. today, completing the last leg of a 16,000-mile round trip trans-Pacific flight to Manila.

The big plane took off from Pearl Harbor, Honolulu, at 5:20 p. m., Pacific Standard Time yesterday.

MANILA, March 9.—Delay of the Philippine Clipper's return trip across the Pacific to Alameda at least until next Saturday was anticipated today because of mechanical difficulties.

KEARNS, PROTEGE SUSPENDED

CHICAGO, March 9.—Jack Kearns and his giant Negro protege, Lorenzo Pack, today were suspended for 30 days by the Illinois Boxing Commission, which said the heavyweight boxer "failed to condition himself properly" for his match two weeks ago with Cowboy Frankie Edgren of Denver.

TROOPS MARCH--STATESMEN PARLEY

When it's 9 p. m. in Berlin and 9 p. m. in Rome

Over in the old world, the news of war is on every lip, the fear of war in every heart. German legions tramp thunderously along the Rhine, and news is made in every capital of Europe, in Washington, in Africa. Because of the difference in time between San Francisco and old world centers, The News gives you the news while it is NEWS. Why wait from 12 to 16 hours to read of events described the SAME day in

THE NEWS

When it's 8 p. m. in London and 3 p. m. in Washington

IT'S NOON IN SAN FRANCISCO

GOLOMBEK FREED, GOES BACK TO NAVY

Eighteen pounds lighter than at the time of his arrest, Henry Golombek, 22-year-old Navy petty officer twice tried for the murder of Helen Tarbox, walked out of the Hall of Justice a free man today.

Superior Judge Lile T. Jacks dismissed the murder charge on recommendation of Dist. Atty. Matthew Brady, who said that because the two trials ended in deadlocks he believed it would be a waste of taxpayers' money to try the youth again.

Golombek ducked out a back door with Chief Petty Officer Charles R. Lowder, who took him to the training station at Yerba Buena Island. Lowder said the murder charge would not be counted against the youth's Navy record.

Heart Problem

What is a girl to do when the Wrong Man stays and the Right Man goes away? Toby Ryan didn't know—but she did a little experimenting, with very satisfying results. Toby is the heroine of "Gorgeous." Watch for it beginning Thursday in

The News

FIG. 15. *The San Francisco News,* March 9, 1936, front page

Tuesday, March 10, 1936 — THE SAN FRANCISCO NEWS — Page 3

REDUCTION IN P. G. E. RATES HELD ILLEGAL

3 Federal Judges Throw Out $2,100,000-a-Year Cut by Rail Board

'CONSTITUTION VIOLATED'

Opinion Based on Method of Determining Cost of Properties

Ragged, Hungry, Broke, Harvest Workers Live in Sqpuallor

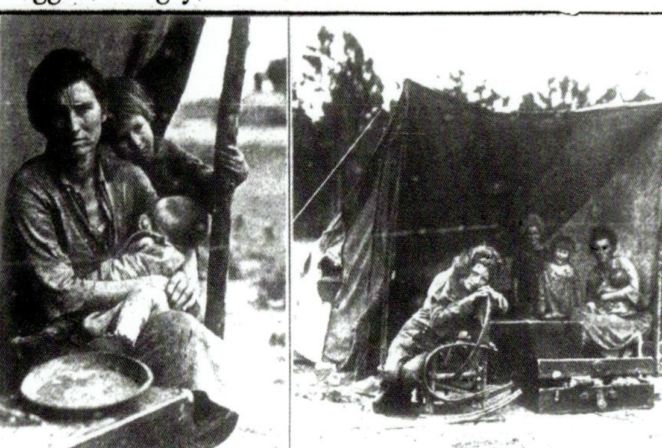

Scores of weary, discouraged and hungry families such as these today awaited the arrival of food at a pea pickers' camp near Nipomo after fighting starvation for six weeks following crop failures.

FOOD RUSHED TO STARVING FARM COLONY

Thousand Jobless Pea Pickers Cheer as Six Weeks of Want Are Ended

WEARY OF LIFE

INCREASE IN ARMY PLANES IS REPORTED

House Committee Approves Boost to 4000 Ships; Air Bases Also Sought

TESTIMONY BY GOFF ATTACKED

Old Police Reports Produced by Defense at Mooney Hearing

My Day By Eleanor Roosevelt

16,440 HARVEST JOBS IN SIGHT

Employment Will Take Care of Discharged WPA Workers, Says McLaughlin

FIG. 16. *The San Francisco News*, March 10, 1936, p. 3

The San Francisco News, Tuesday, March 10, 1936

RAGGED, HUNGRY, BROKE, HARVEST WORKERS LIVE IN SQUALLOR [*sic*]

"Scores of weary, discouraged and hungry families such as these today awaited the arrival of food at a pea pickers' camp near Nipomo after fighting starvation for six weeks following crop failures."

FOOD RUSHED TO STARVING FARM COLONY

Thousand Jobless Pea Pickers Cheer as Six Weeks of Want Are Ended

NIPOMO, March 10.—A ragged army of pea pickers set up a faint cheer today at news that the Federal Government is rushing them supplies of food to ward off the threat of starvation.

Faces of destitute field workers, stranded by a crop failure, brightened when a United Press correspondent brought word that 20,000 pounds of food were en route here from Los Angeles.

"How we need it!" exclaimed J. W. Carpenter, the camp boss. [. . .]

Previous reports that San Luis Obispo County had been caring for them were denied by Mr. Carpenter, a former Little Rock, Ark., resident who came West many months ago to join the nomadic army of workers who follow the seasonal pea crops from the Imperial Valley to Idaho.

Two Days Work in Six Weeks

Mr. Carpenter insisted the workers had been left to shift for themselves.

"We have been keeping body and soul together by taking cauliflower and whatever other kind of vegetables we can get from neighboring fields," he said. [. . .] "We have worked only two days in six weeks. We got an average of about 75¢ each for the two days. That's all the money we've seen and we've been here six weeks. It'll be three or five weeks more before the new crop comes in."

Tires Sold for Food

Mr. Carpenter said the camp originally was much larger. But when the blight set in, those that could moved on. The others had no money to buy gasoline for their ramshackle cars. A number of these ancient cars were stripped to their rims, bearing out Mr. Carpenter's statement that their owners had sold the tires to get money for food. Clothes and even bedding were disposed of for the same purpose, the camp boss related. [. . .]

On March 11 the *San Francisco News* ran a follow-up editorial, "What Does the 'New Deal' Mean To This Mother and Her Children?" illustrated with Lange's *Migrant Mother*—the first of innumerable reproductions to come **[FIG. 17]**. United Press coverage of the plight of the migrant workers—often accompanied by her photographs—appeared in more than a dozen papers across California over the following weeks. Lange, who was typically very conscientious about her field notes, had been rushing home on that fateful day; none of the notes she submitted with this batch of negatives refer to these photographs. To make up

The San Francisco News,
Wednesday, March 11, 1936

WHAT DOES THE 'NEW DEAL' MEAN TO THIS MOTHER AND HER CHILDREN?

This remarkable photograph epitomizes the human side of one of California's oldest and gravest problems—the plight of nearly 200,000 men, women and children who move from valley to valley with the crops and live in wretched improvised shelters as they perform the labor on which our harvests depend.

Here, in the fine strong face of this mother, photographed at the camp of starving pea-pickers in San Luis Obispo County, is the tragedy of lives lived in squalor and fear, on terms that mock the American dream of security and independence and opportunity in which every child has been taught to believe.

The shame is that California is not only not tackling this problem but that through its wealthiest and most responsible citizens it is deliberately seeking to block the one constructive step that has been proposed to make life a little more secure and a little more decent for these people. We refer to the desire of the Federal Resettlement Administration to build 20 sanitary camps for migratory workers, and to the organized opposition of the agricultural section of the State Chamber of Congress to the carrying out of that program.

The conscience of California should find its voice in a demand that the Federal Government be encouraged to go ahead with its plans for these sorely needed camps.

1800 RAGGED HARVESTERS GET FIRST SQUARE MEAL

[. . .] They have been subsisting on stolen vegetables, raked from nearby farms at night, and a few birds killed by children. [. . .]

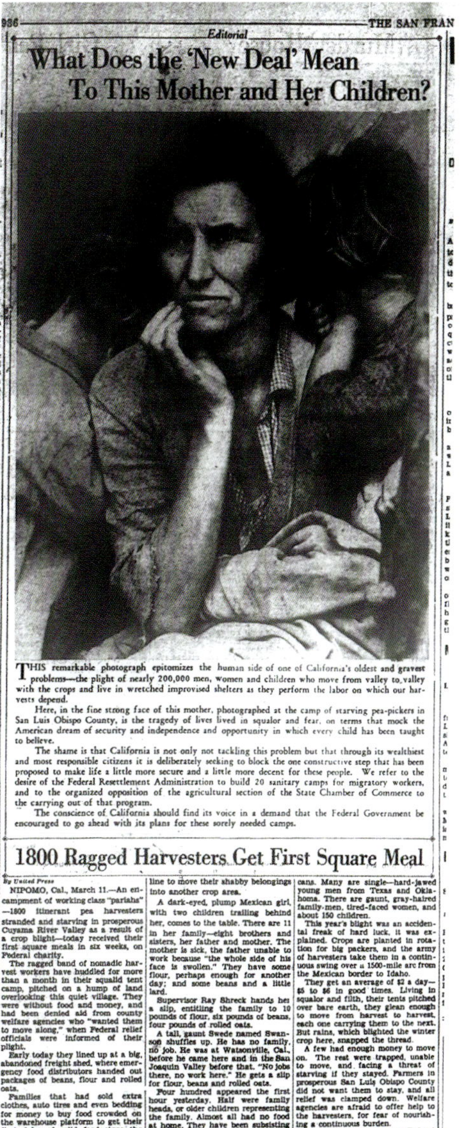

936 THE SAN FRAN

Editorial

What Does the 'New Deal' Mean To This Mother and Her Children?

THIS remarkable photograph epitomizes the human side of one of California's oldest and gravest problems—the plight of nearly 200,000 men, women and children who move from valley to valley with the crops and live in wretched improvised shelters as they perform the labor on which our harvests depend.

Here, in the fine strong face of this mother, photographed at the camp of starving pea-pickers in San Luis Obispo County, is the tragedy of lives lived in squalor and fear, on terms that mock the American dream of security and independence and opportunity in which every child has been taught to believe.

The shame is that California is not only not tackling this problem but that through its wealthiest and most responsible citizens it is deliberately seeking to block the one constructive step that has been proposed to make life a little more secure and a little more decent for these people. We refer to the desire of the Federal Resettlement Administration to build 20 sanitary camps for migratory workers, and to the organized opposition of the agricultural section of the State Chamber of Commerce to the carrying out of that program.

The conscience of California should find its voice in a demand that the Federal Government be encouraged to go ahead with its plans for these sorely needed camps.

1800 Ragged Harvesters Get First Square Meal

By United Press

NIPOMO, Cal., March 11.—An encampment of working class "pariahs"—1800 itinerant pea harvesters stranded and starving in prosperous Cuyama River Valley as a result of a crop blight—today received their first square meals in six weeks, on Federal charity.

The ragged band of nomadic harvest workers have huddled for more than a month in their squalid tent camp, pitched on a hump of land overlooking this quiet village. They were without food and money, and had been denied aid from county welfare agencies who "wanted them to move along," when Federal relief officials were informed of their plight.

Early today they lined up at a big, abandoned freight shed, where emergency food distributors handed out packages of beans, flour and rolled oats.

Families that had sold extra clothes, auto tires and even bedding for money to buy food crowded on the warehouse platform to get their first doles of solid food since the rainy season ravaged the pea crop with "rust" blight, leaving the imported pea pickers without jobs and without money to buy enough gasoline to move their shabby belongings into another crop area.

A dark-eyed, plump Mexican girl, with two children trailing behind her, comes to the table. There are 11 in her family—eight brothers and sisters, her father and mother. The mother is sick, the father unable to work because "the whole side of his face is swollen." They have some flour, perhaps enough for another day; and some beans and a little lard.

Supervisor Ray Shreck hands her a slip, entitling the family to 10 pounds of flour, six pounds of beans, four pounds of rolled oats.

A tall, gaunt Swede named Swanson shuffles up. He has no family, no job. He was at Watsonville, Cal., before he came here and in the San Joaquin Valley before that. "No jobs there, no work here." He gets a slip for flour, beans and rolled oats.

Four hundred appeared the first hour yesterday. Half were family heads, or older children representing the family. Almost all had no food at home. They have been subsisting on stolen vegetables, raked from nearby farms at night, and a few birds killed by children.

Six camps sprawl over the slope behind the town. About 800 in the camps are Americans, the rest Mexicans. Many are single—hard-jawed young men from Texas and Oklahoma. There are gaunt, gray-haired family-men, tired-faced women, and about 150 children.

This year's blight was an accidental freak of hard luck, it was explained. Crops are planted in rotation for big packers, and the army of harvesters take them in a continuous swing over a 1500-mile arc from the Mexican border to Idaho.

They get an average of $2 a day—$5 to $6 in good times. Living in squalor and filth, their tents pitched over bare earth, they glean enough to move from harvest to harvest, each one carrying them to the next. But rains, which blighted the winter crop here, snapped the thread.

A few had enough money to move on. The rest were trapped, unable to move, and facing a threat of starving if they stayed. Farmers in prosperous San Luis Obispo County did not want them to stay, and all relief was clamped down. Welfare agencies are afraid to offer help to the harvesters, for fear of nourishing a continuous burden.

Only the accident of a Federal survey photographer's report drew attention of Federal relief officials, and resulted in food being trucked to the camp from Los Angeles yesterday.

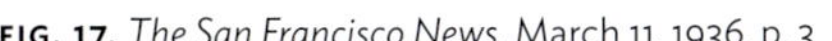

FIG. 17. *The San Francisco News*, March 11, 1936, p. 3

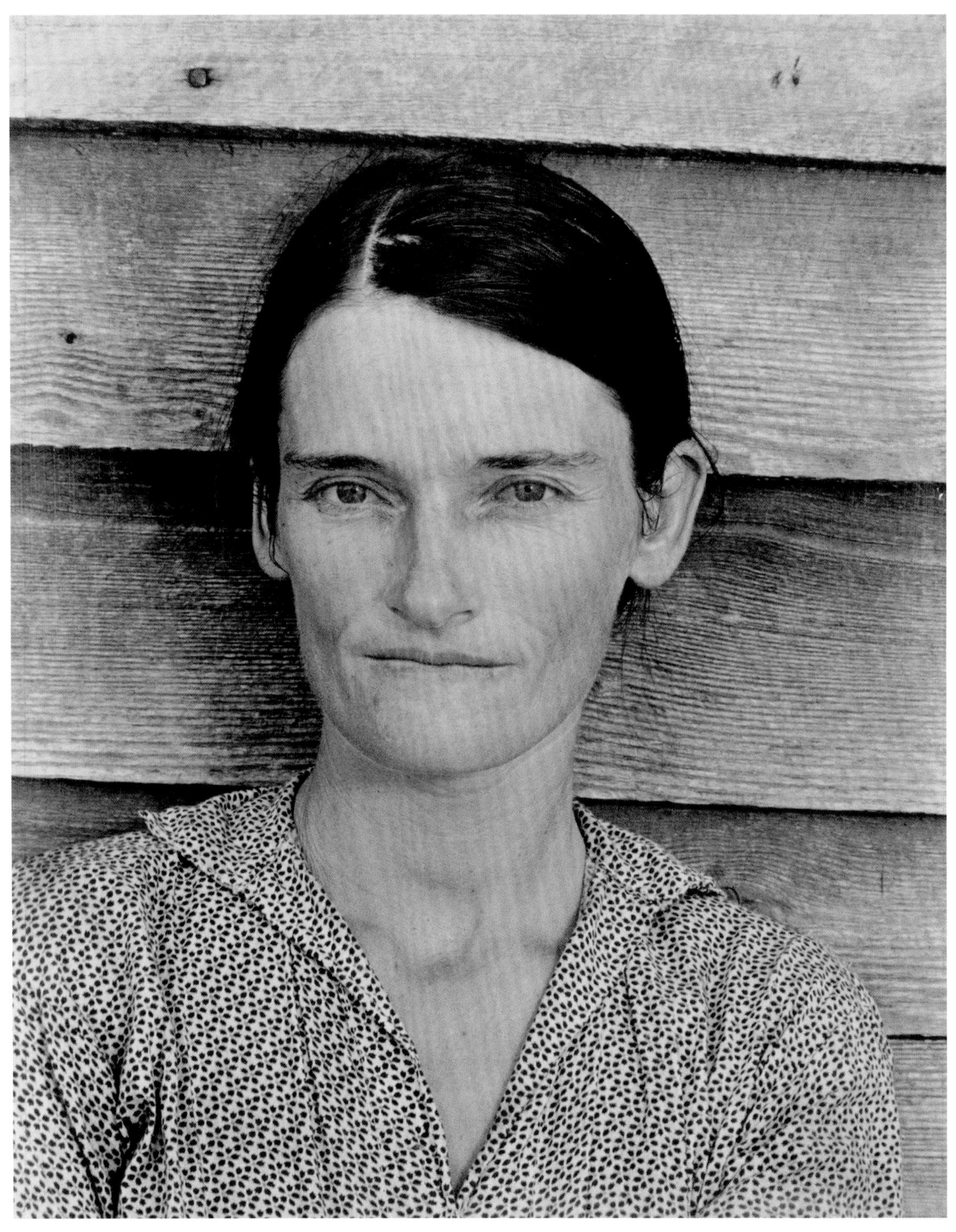

FIG. 18. Walker Evans (American, 1903–1975). *Alabama Cotton Tenant Farmer Wife (Allie Mae Burroughs).* 1936. Gelatin silver print, 8 11⁄16 x 7" (22.1 x 17.8 cm). THE MUSEUM OF MODERN ART, NEW YORK. GIFT OF THE ARTIST (PROMOTED 2015)

for their absence, it appears that the published newspaper reports were distilled into captions for the series, which explains why they do not perfectly align with the images. To this day, these captions accompany Lange's photographs from the series on the file cards in the Library of Congress, and (with some variations) are provided whenever the images are accessed. It would be many years before *Migrant Mother* came to be known as such.

Lange's photographs were at the heart of two important photobooks from this era: The first was Archibald MacLeish's 1938 *Land of the Free*, described by its author in the volume's notes section as "the opposite of a book of poems illustrated by photographs. It is a book of photographs illustrated by a poem." More than a third of its photographs are by Lange, including *Migrant Mother*. The second photobook was Lange and Taylor's *An American Exodus: A Record of Human Erosion*, published the following year. *Migrant Mother* is not among its 112 reproductions, perhaps reflecting the authors' sense that Lange's other achievements had already been eclipsed by this one. Roy Stryker, head of the FSA's photographic division, would later reflect: "When Dorothea took that picture, that was the ultimate. She never surpassed it. To me, it was *the* picture of Farm Security. The others were marvelous but that was special. . . . I'll stand on that picture as long as I live."[21]

Stryker's praise is all the more notable given the many other talented photographers associated with the FSA, including Walker Evans, Russell Lee, Arthur Rothstein, Ben Shahn, and Marion Post Wolcott. The comparison between Lange and Evans is particularly significant, as their talents are comparable, although their sensibilities and motivations were very different. In Alabama in 1936, Evans made the FSA photograph that rivals *Migrant Mother* in its iconic power **[FIG. 18]**. John Szarkowski—the longtime Director of the Department of Photography at MoMA, who organized retrospectives of both Lange and Evans—compared their experiences working for Stryker as follows:

> Evans did not so much challenge Stryker's authority as ignore it; he was not interested in photography as a method of political persuasion, but was delighted to be paid by the federal government to make his own pictures, as long as they wished to do so. Clearly, Evans had an attitude problem, but he was not really a threat to Stryker's role. . . . Lange, on the other hand, shared without reservation Stryker's belief in photography as a tool of political education (propaganda), and brought to the belief a more passionate enthusiasm, a larger ego, [and] at least as keen an intelligence.[22]

When Lange encountered Thompson, the photographer was the mother of two sons (ages seven and ten), as well as four stepchildren from Taylor's and Dixon's first marriages. Lange was separated from her children sometimes for

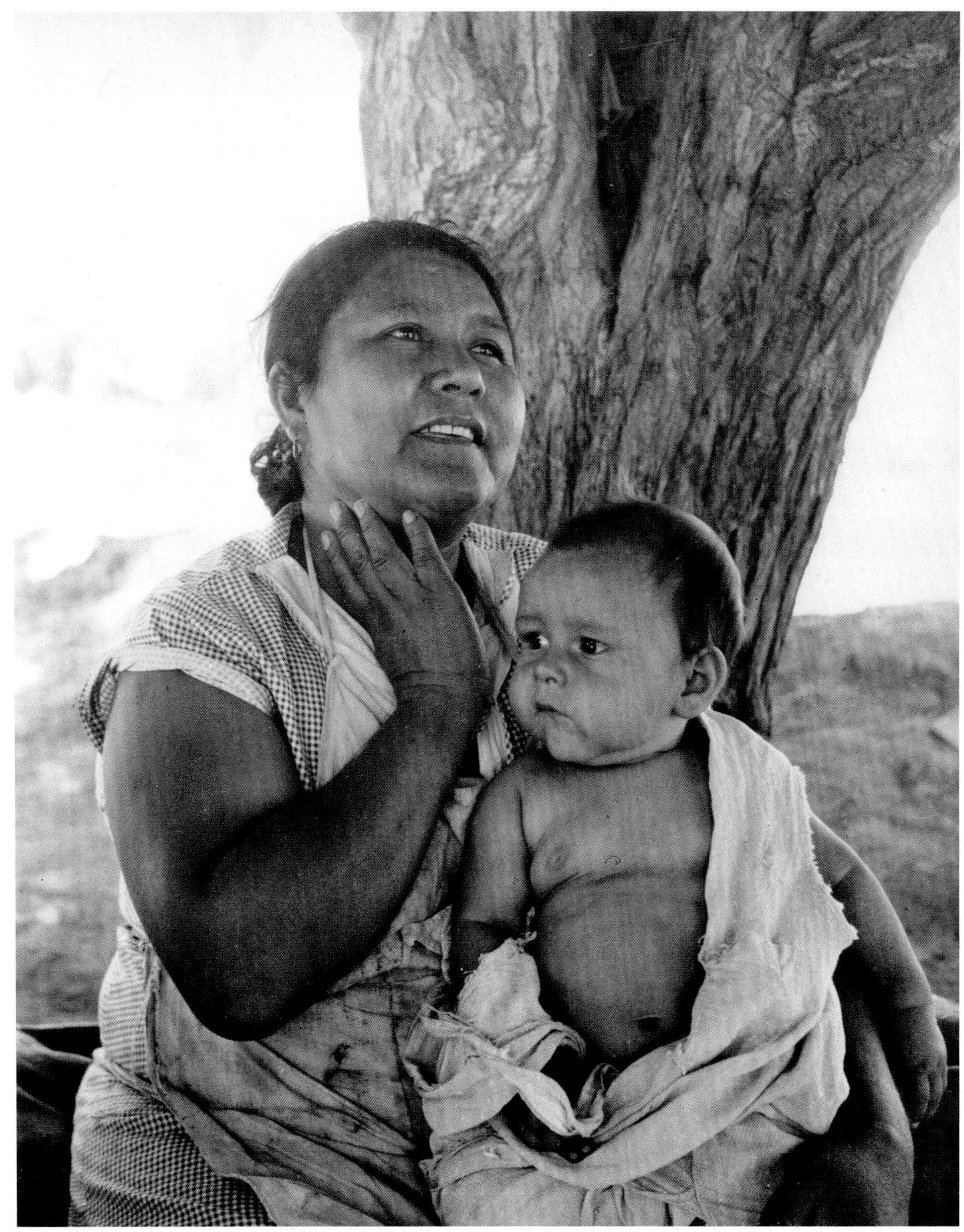

FIG. 19. Dorothea Lange (American, 1895–1965). "Mexican Mother in California. 'Sometimes I tell my children that I would like to go to Mexico, but they tell me "We don't want to go, we belong here."' (Note on Mexican labor situation in repatriation.)" June 1935. Digital file from 4 x 5" (10.2 x 12.7 cm) negative. FARM SECURITY ADMINISTRATION–OFFICE OF WAR INFORMATION PHOTOGRAPH COLLECTION, LIBRARY OF CONGRESS

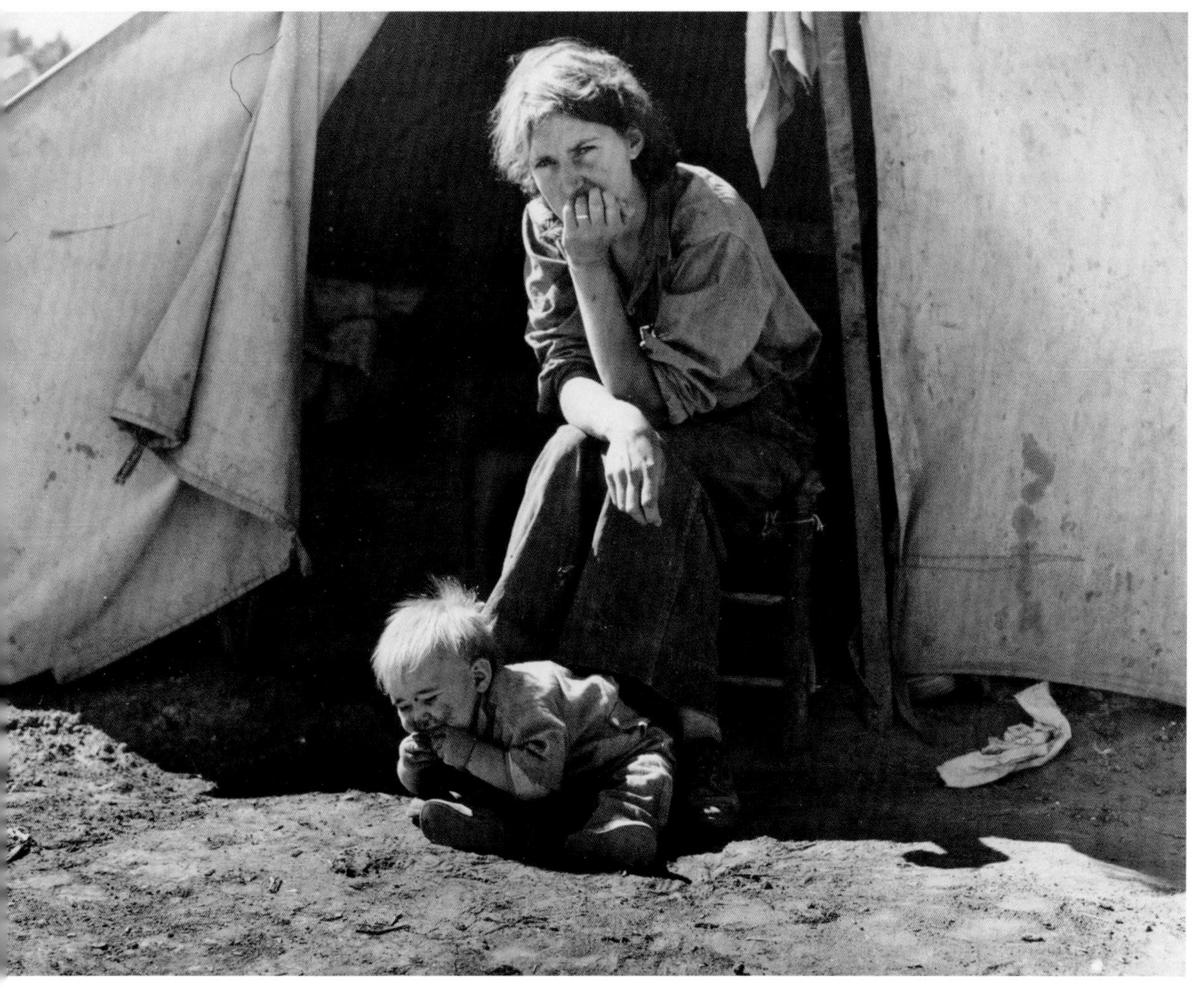

FIG. 20. Dorothea Lange (American, 1895–1965). *Young Mother, a Migrant, California.* March 1937. Gelatin silver print, 7 ⅝ x 8 ⅝" (19.4 x 21.9 cm). THE MUSEUM OF MODERN ART, NEW YORK. GIFT OF THE FARM SECURITY ADMINISTRATION, 1941

weeks at a time: economic hardship had forced her and Dixon to board their sons out to a more affluent family (not an uncommon practice during the Depression); and after she met Taylor, their field trips often drew her away from home. Decades later, she would reflect: "Even now when I speak of it I can feel the pain. It hurts me in the same place as it did then."[23] This personal struggle—inflected by the exalted position of maternal figures in the American social landscape, and the centuries-old connections to images of the Madonna and Child—begin to explain the centrality of the theme of motherhood in Lange's work **[FIGS. 19, 20]**.[24]

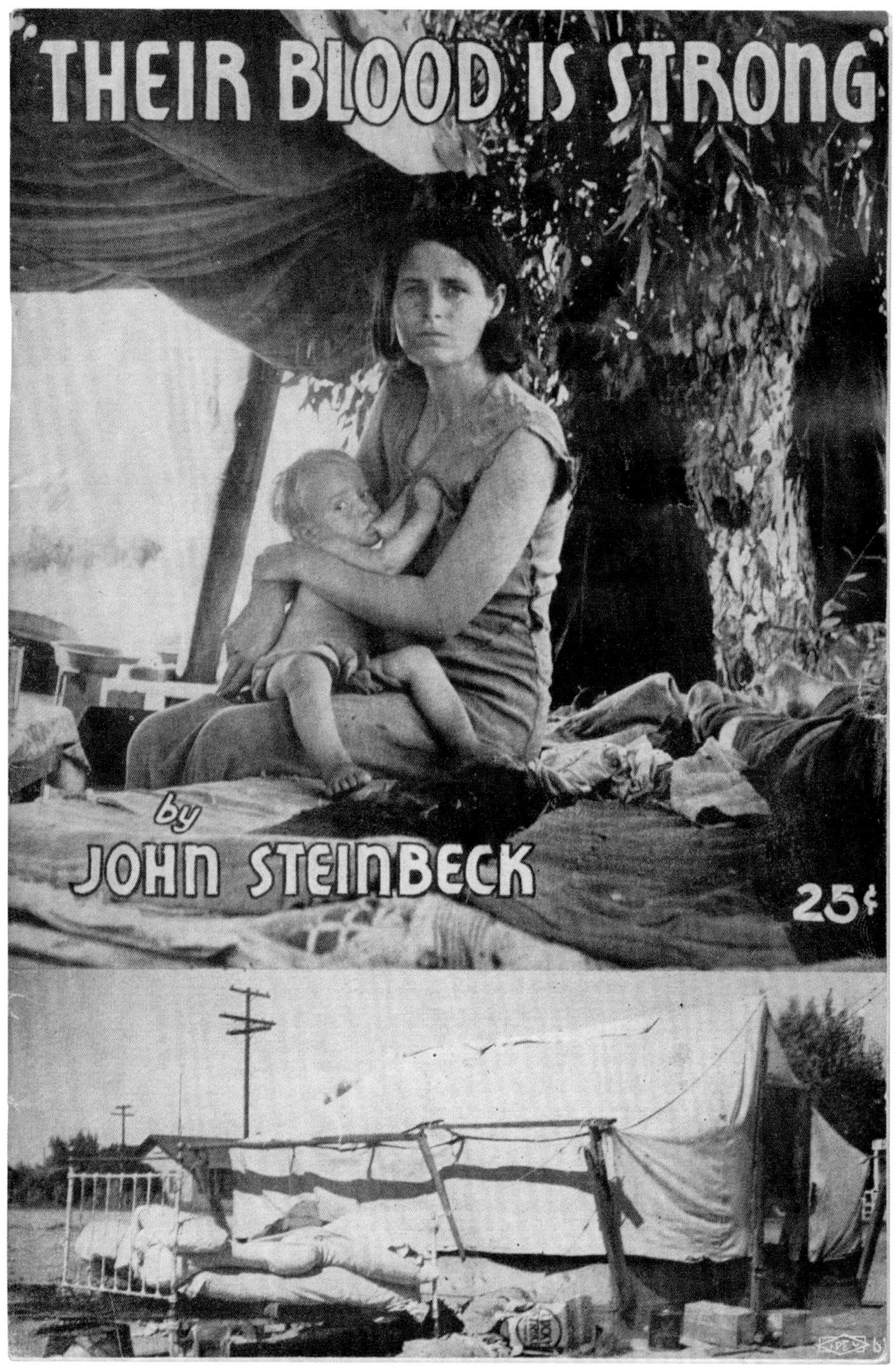

FIG. 21. John Steinbeck's *Their Blood Is Strong* (San Francisco: Simon J. Lubin Society of California, April 1938). Cover photographs by Dorothea Lange. RARE BOOK & MANUSCRIPT LIBRARY, COLUMBIA UNIVERSITY, NEW YORK

Attuned to this profound symbolic power, the editors of the *San Francisco News* reproduced one of Lange's photographs from the Migrant Mother suite **[SEE FIG. 14]**, cropped into a vertical, on October 5, 1936, alongside the first installment of "The Harvest Gypsies," a series of articles on California's migrant workers by John Steinbeck. These writings solidified Steinbeck's standing as an authority on the Dust Bowl migration in California, more than two years before the publication of his novel *The Grapes of Wrath*. The articles were gathered into a pamphlet in 1938, published under the title *Their Blood Is Strong* and illustrated with photographs by Lange **[FIG. 21]**. As the historian James R. Swensen has pointed out, *Migrant Mother* and *The Grapes of Wrath* have both come to represent the Great Depression for generations that did not experience it firsthand.[25] Perhaps not coincidentally, both works are anchored in a maternal figure.

The identity of the Migrant Mother remained unknown to the millions who encountered the photograph until 1978, when reports circulated via the Associated Press that Thompson felt exploited and intimated that she should have been somehow compensated for her role in the famous photograph, threatening a lawsuit to anyone who persisted in publishing it.[26] This hostility waned in August 1983 when her children's plea for help offsetting Thompson's medical costs (first published in the *San Jose Mercury News*) brought a reported $30,000 from thousands of strangers who had been touched by Lange's photograph over the decades.[27]

In 1978 it was also revealed that Thompson was in fact Cherokee, not of European descent (as had been assumed by Lange and many others), introducing the question of how race affects our reading of this image.[28] Art historian Sally Stein reflects:

> There is something to be said for thinking that the ethnicity of the central subject in this revered picture should not matter, especially because in the past it never seemed to matter. Downplaying the belated revelation of Migrant Mother's Native American identity may serve as proof that our society is moving close to a state of color blindness. Then again, can the eradication of racism ever be achieved if we ignore the racialized ground on which the nation established itself and continually expanded?[29]

Surely the assumption that Thompson was white has been a factor in the reception of this photograph that we can no longer ignore. Would the image's iconic power have been as far-reaching had Thompson been seen as nonwhite? We cannot know, but it must be said that Lange (and Taylor) had an equitable concern for itinerant workers of all races **[SEE FIGS. 6 AND 19]** that was uncommon for the era, and indeed for today.

—

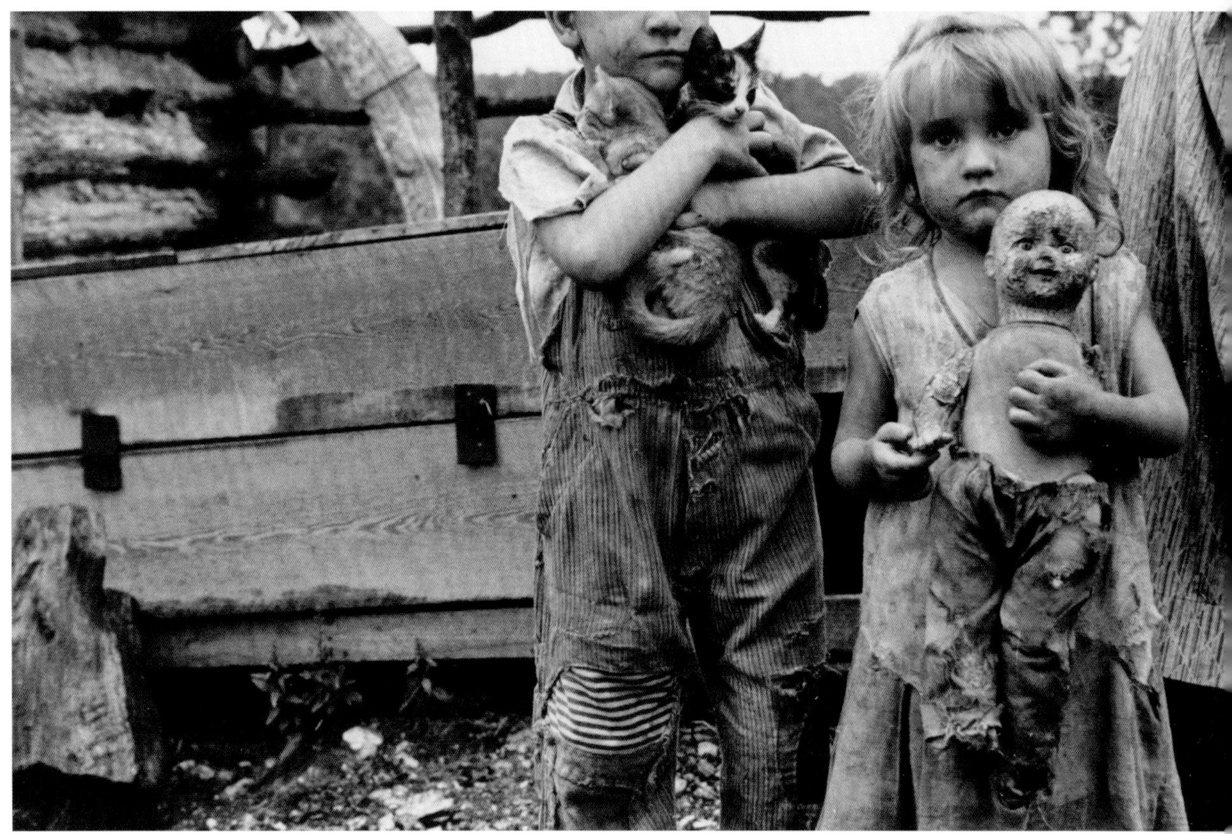

FIG. 22. Ben Shahn (American, born Lithuania, 1898–1969). *Children of Destitute Mountaineer*. 1935. Gelatin silver print, 6 ½ x 9 ⅝" (16.5 x 24.4 cm). THE MUSEUM OF MODERN ART, NEW YORK. GIFT OF THE FARM SECURITY ADMINISTRATION, 1941

It is possible, even likely, that *Migrant Mother* has been exhibited at The Museum of Modern Art more often than any other photograph in the Museum's collection. It was first shown in the Department of Photography's inaugural exhibition, *Sixty Photographs: A Survey of Camera Esthetics*, which opened December 31, 1940. In the members' bulletin that served as a catalogue for the show, *Migrant Mother* was one of seven photographs featured as a full-page reproduction (its title was given there as *Pea Picker Family, California, 1936*). In the exhibition it was presented on a panel alongside works by Alfred Stieglitz, Eugène Atget, and Paul Strand—distinguished company, to be sure.

The first print of *Migrant Mother*—there would be several—to enter the Museum's collection was acquired in 1940: one of six Lange photographs given by the San Francisco–based collector Albert M. Bender. It was this print that was exhibited in *Sixty Photographs*, and its acquisition was part of the Museum's concerted effort in the late 1930s and early 1940s to expand its photography holdings. Perhaps because of Bender's gift, *Migrant Mother* was not among the more than sixty prints acquired as gifts from the Farm Security Administration between 1938 and 1941; the Museum and the FSA must have realized the mutual advantages in such an arrangement **[FIGS. 22, 23]**. *Sixty Photographs* did not, however, mark the first occasion on which this photograph by Lange was displayed in an artistic context: as early as September 1936, *Migrant Mother* was included in substantial exhibitions organized by U.S. Camera and the College Art Association, and in April 1938 her work was "beautifully represented" in the First International Photographic Exposition, held at New York's Grand Central Palace, which featured at least a dozen prints by Lange **[FIG. 24]**.[30] MoMA's own Department of Circulating Exhibitions assumed responsibility for touring fifty FSA photographs

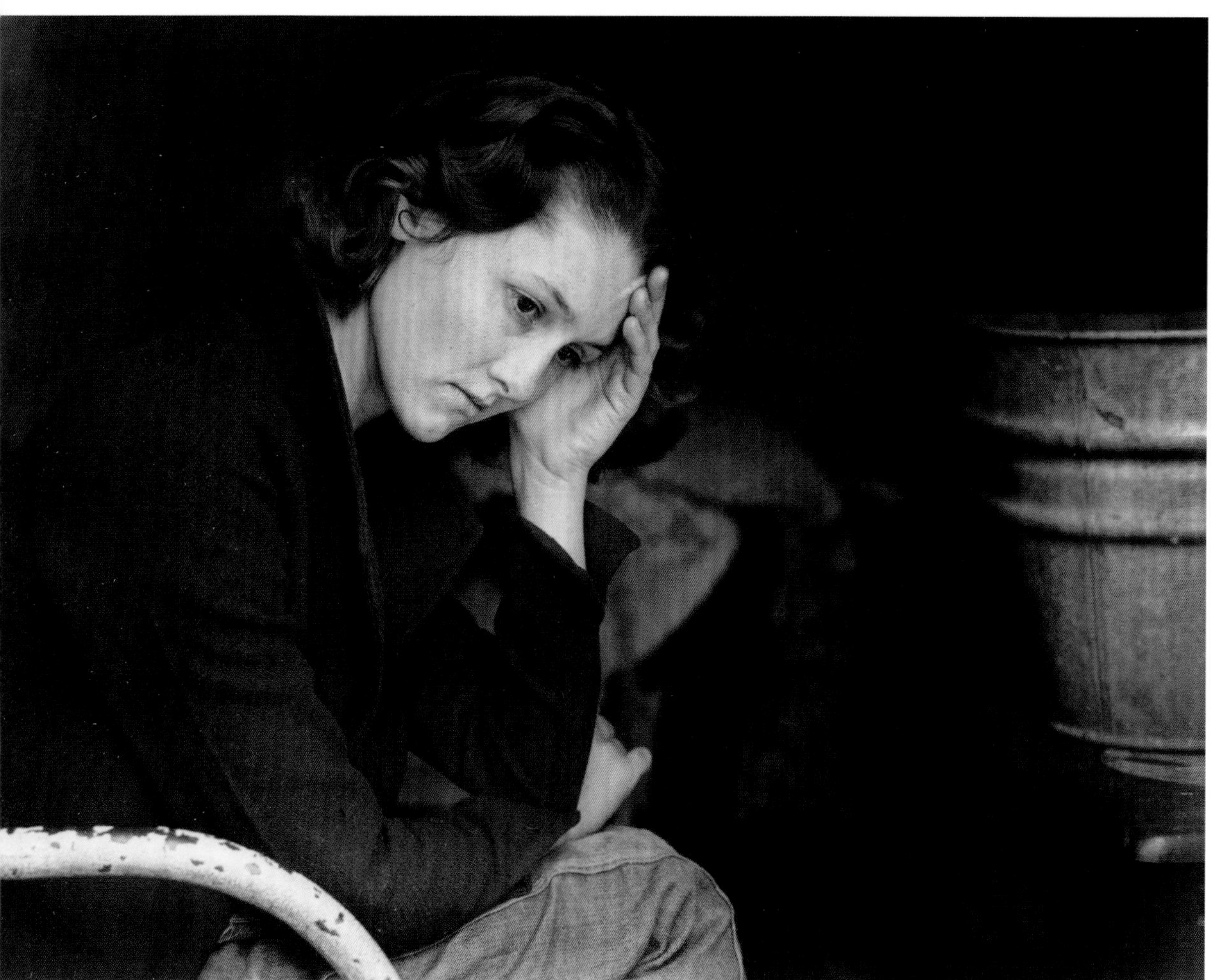

FIG. 23. Dorothea Lange (American, 1895–1965). *Daughter of Migrant Tennessee Coal Miner Living in American River Camp near Sacramento*. 1936. Gelatin silver print, 7 ½ x 9 ½" (19.1 x 24.1 cm). THE MUSEUM OF MODERN ART, NEW YORK. GIFT OF THE FARM SECURITY ADMINISTRATION, 1938

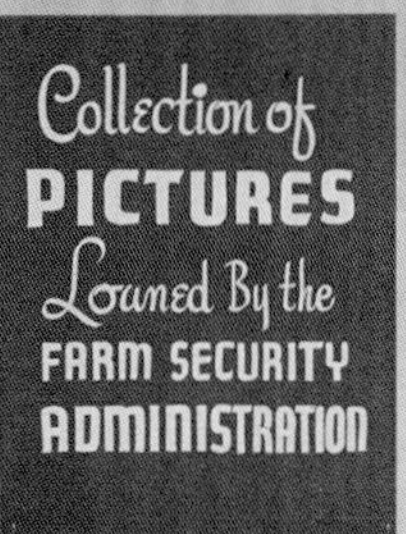

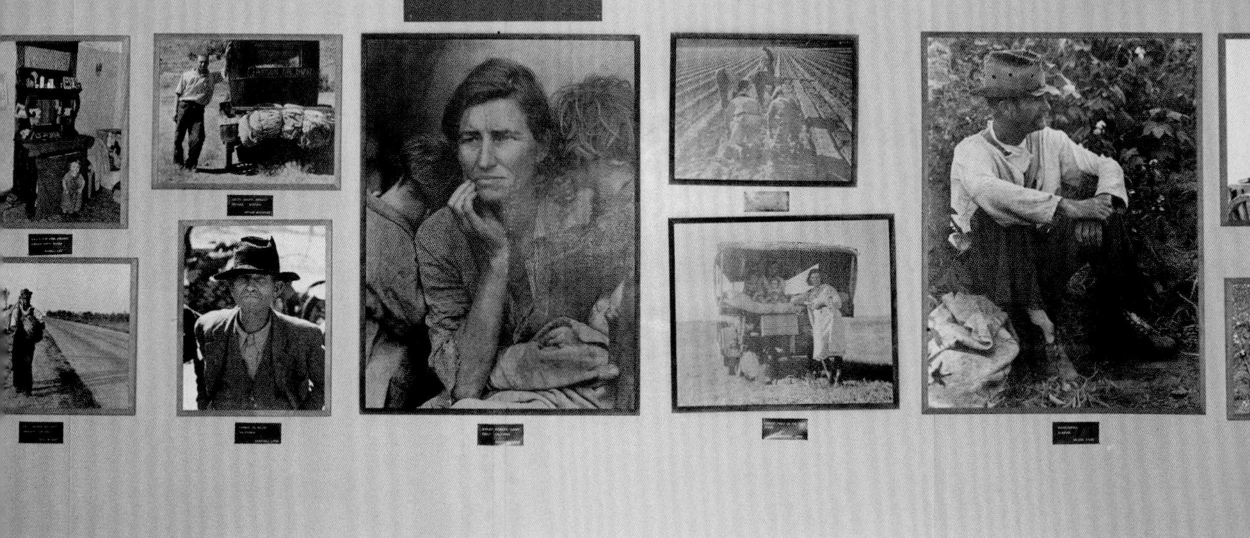

FIG. 24. Installation view of the First International Photographic Exposition, Grand Central Palace, New York, April 18–29, 1938. *Migrant Mother*, here captioned "Migrant Worker's Hungry Family, California," is beneath the title panel. Photograph by Arthur Rothstein. FARM SECURITY ADMINISTRATION–OFFICE OF WAR INFORMATION PHOTOGRAPH COLLECTION, LIBRARY OF CONGRESS

drawn from that show as its own exhibition, titled *Documents of America*, in 1939 and 1940.[31]

After its MoMA debut in *Sixty Photographs*, the print of *Migrant Mother* that Bender had donated was displayed regularly at the Museum.[32] Alas, on September 12, 1952, less than a month after the print's inclusion in an exhibition titled *Then and Now*, the Museum's registrar wrote a memo to Edward Steichen, then Director of the Department of Photography, that opens: "Dear Captain Steichen: The Museum Collection photographs which disappeared from your offices on August 20th [two days after *Then and Now* closed] are insured for the following valuations."[33] Bender's *Migrant Mother* (insured for $10) was one of the missing photographs; that print was never recovered.

Despite *Migrant Mother*'s many iterations, even at MoMA, this book is part of a series—One on One—and there is a single print to which this "one" refers **[FRONTISPIECE, INSIDE BACK COVER FOLDOUT]**. It was mounted on Masonite and included in *Six Women Photographers* at MoMA in 1949. It subsequently traveled internationally as part of *Contemporary American Photography*, prepared by

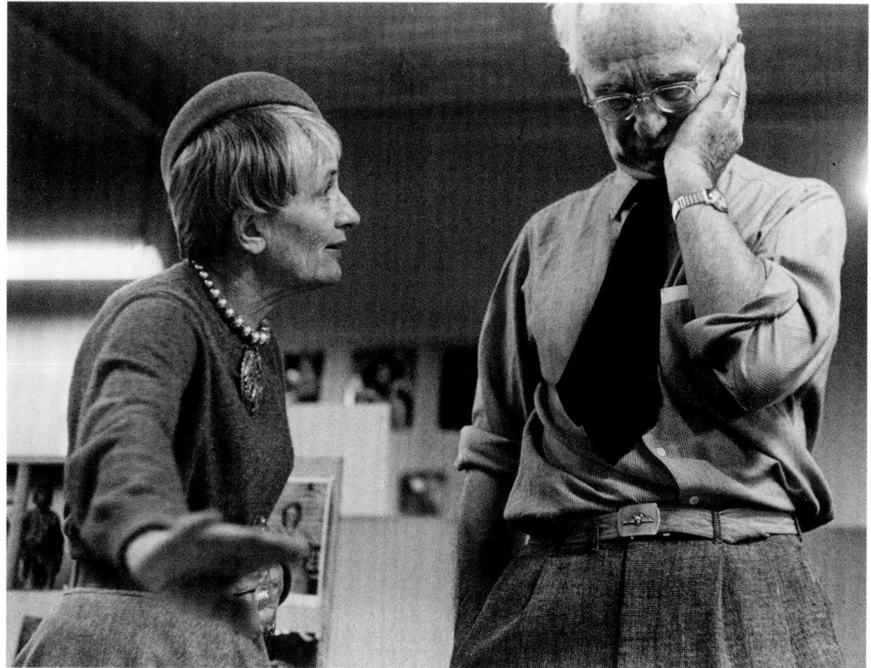

FIG. 25. Dorothea Lange and Edward Steichen working on *The Family of Man*. 1952. Photograph by Homer Page. THE MUSEUM OF MODERN ART ARCHIVES, NEW YORK

Steichen for the Museum. The cropping is a bit more generous than the FSA file image, and the print is slightly lighter, although still somber. The most notable difference is that Thompson's left thumb holding the tent pole is barely visible. Lange found the thumb distracting and had an assistant retouch the negative in 1939—to Stryker's horror: for Stryker, authenticity was paramount, and any tampering with the negative undermined the photograph's integrity as an honest document.[34]

Lange traveled to New York in September 1952, ostensibly to meet with Steichen and discuss a selection of her work for the forthcoming exhibition *Diogenes with a Camera II*. They surely spent more time talking about *The Family of Man*, Steichen's landmark exhibition that used "the simple direct terms of photography" to mirror the "essential goodness and oneness of man."[35] Lange played an important role not only in soliciting contributions from West Coast photographers for that project, but more broadly in shaping the concept of the exhibition **[FIG. 25]**.[36] Lange and Steichen shared a belief that pictures could communicate as clearly as words, and that multiple images, when combined with

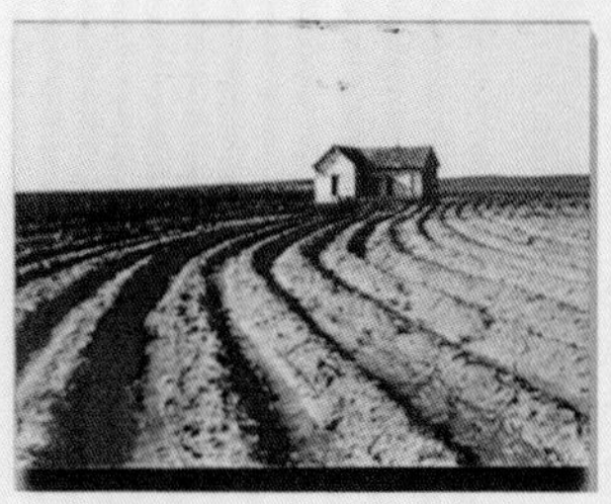
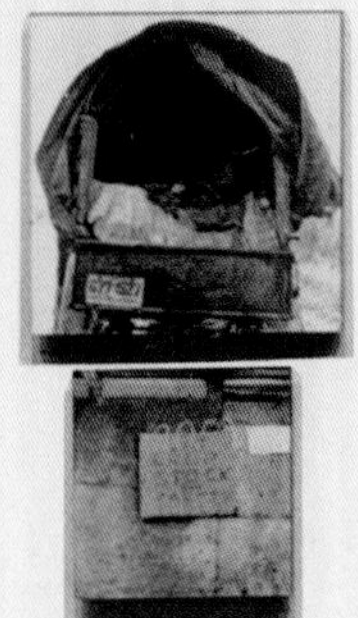
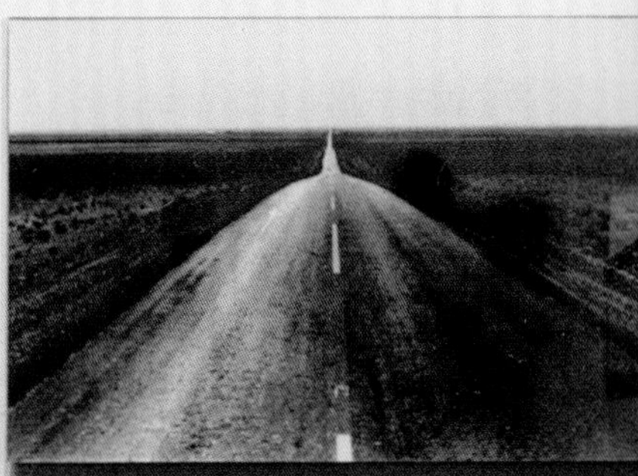

FIG. 26. Installation view of *Dorothea Lange*, The Museum of Modern Art, New York, January 26–April 10, 1966. Photograph by Rolf Petersen. THE MUSEUM OF MODERN ART ARCHIVES, NEW YORK

sensitivity and intelligence, could construct sentences, paragraphs, even essays. And conversely, they both understood that written words could clarify the meaning of photographs. Steichen included nine of Lange's photographs in *The Family of Man*, *Migrant Mother* among them. In 1962, in *The Bitter Years: 1935–1941*—the final exhibition he would organize for MoMA—Steichen featured no fewer than eighty-five works by her, again including *Migrant Mother*.[37]

It was Steichen's successor at MoMA, though, who organized Lange's first major retrospective. Indeed, respect for her work was one of few things John Szarkowski shared with Steichen. Szarkowski titled his first exhibition as Director of MoMA's Department of Photography *Five Unrelated Photographers* (1963),

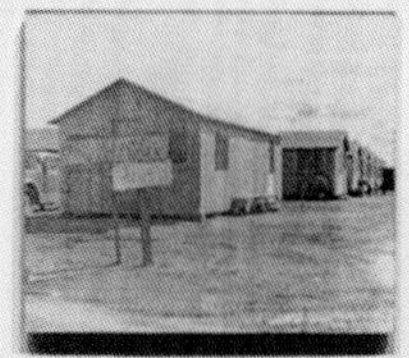

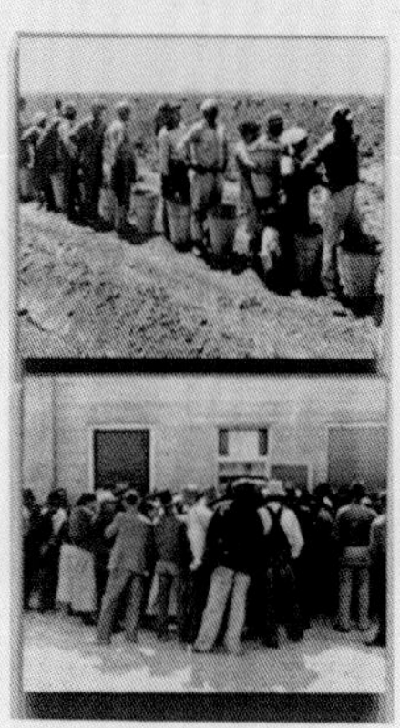

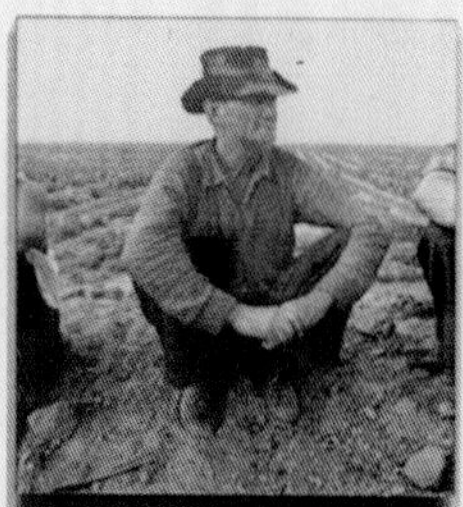

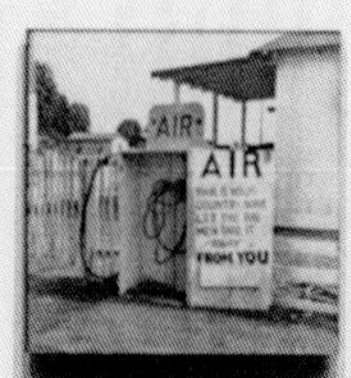

and the press release might fairly be characterized as a rebuttal to *The Family of Man*: "The exhibition does not *include* their work, it is *of* it. No attempt is made to link them together with a central theme or idea."[38] Less than a year later, Szarkowski would write to Lange that he had put her retrospective on the exhibition calendar, "whether you like it or not."[39] Thus began their collaboration for her first retrospective as an artist, and his first as a curator. Unfortunately, Lange would not live to see the results: she died October 11, 1965; the exhibition opened to the public January 26, 1966 **[FIG. 26]**.

—

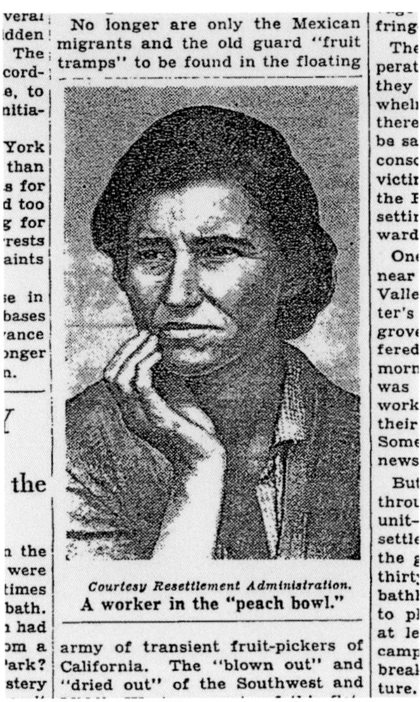
No longer are only the Mexican migrants and the old guard "fruit tramps" to be found in the floating

Courtesy Resettlement Administration.
A worker in the "peach bowl."

army of transient fruit-pickers of California. The "blown out" and "dried out" of the Southwest and

FIG. 27. *Migrant Mother,* as published in the *New York Times,* August 30, 1936, p. X9

Claims of "truth" in photography can be complicated. Even in the pre-digital era, it was a simple enough matter to alter a photograph, stretching (or even rupturing) its relationship to whatever had appeared before the camera's lens.[40] Years before Lange and Stryker disagreed about the "glaring defect" she had removed from the *Migrant Mother* negative (Thompson's thumb),[41] the *New York Times* had published a version of the image in which the *children* had been removed, and the dingy interior of the tent made to appear as wisps of clouds in a bright sky **[FIG. 27]**. The Museum owns another heavily retouched print of *Migrant Mother* that was published in the *Times* on July 26, 1936 **[FIG. 28]**.[42] The manipulation seems to have been intended to improve the image's legibility: heightening the contrast between figure and background, accentuating the outlines, and clumsily but effectively minimizing the presence of Thompson's offending thumb. Stryker's fear that changes such as these would undermine the government's (and the public's) willingness to accept Lange's photograph as an accurate representation of the impact of the Great Depression has proved to be unfounded. *Migrant Mother* is more than fact; the image has taken on legendary status.

That status was irresistible to the editors of *Popular Photography*, who, in April 2005, published an "improved" *Migrant Mother* as an April Fool's joke **[FIG. 29]**. They mimicked some of the 1936 edits from the *New York Times* ("First,

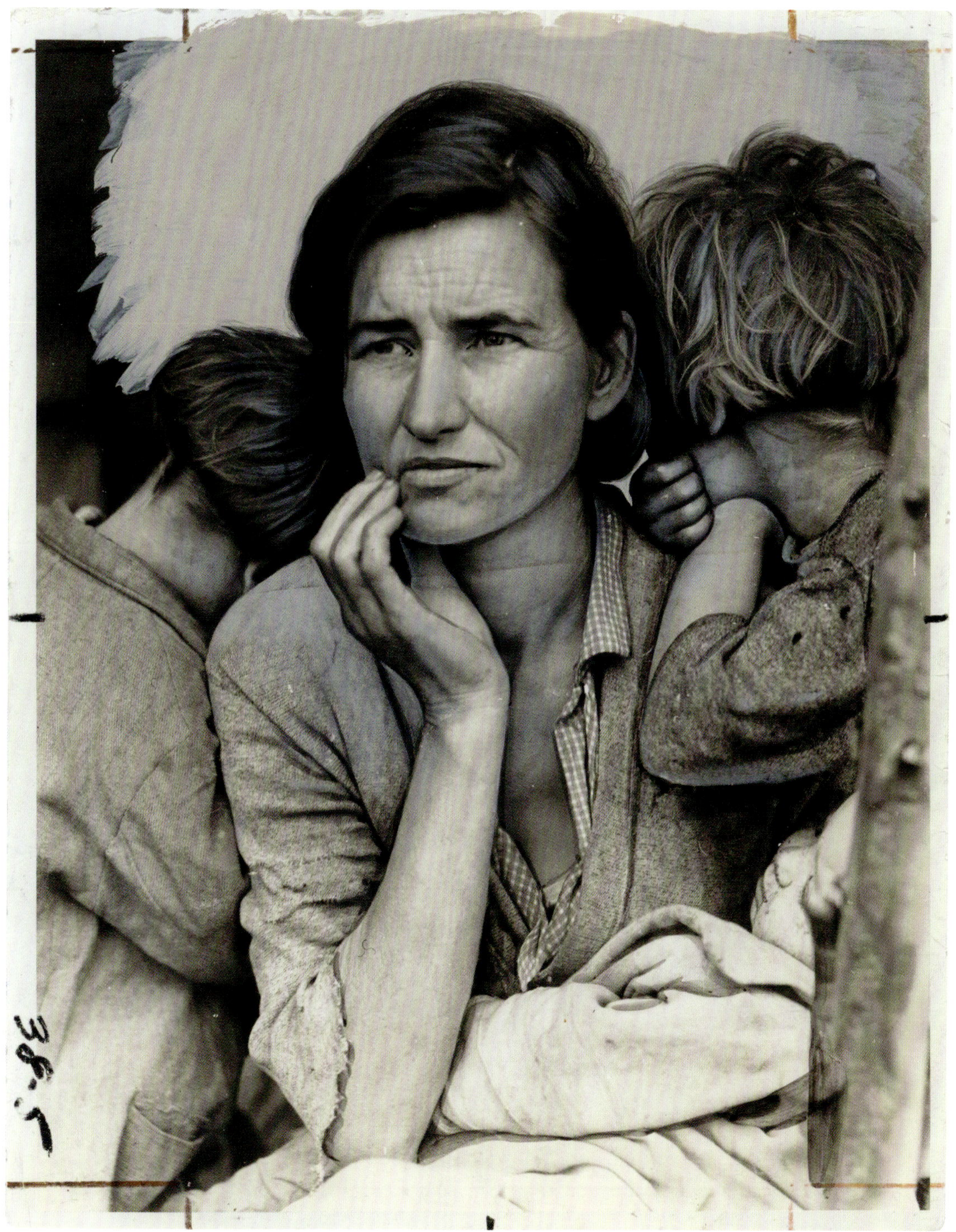

FIG. 28. Dorothea Lange (American, 1895–1965). "A Destitute Mother: The Type Aided by the WPA." Gelatin silver print with gouache (painted and airbrushed), ink and grease pencil, 10 x 7 11/16" (25.5 x 19.6 cm). THE MUSEUM OF MODERN ART, NEW YORK. THE NEW YORK TIMES COLLECTION, 2001

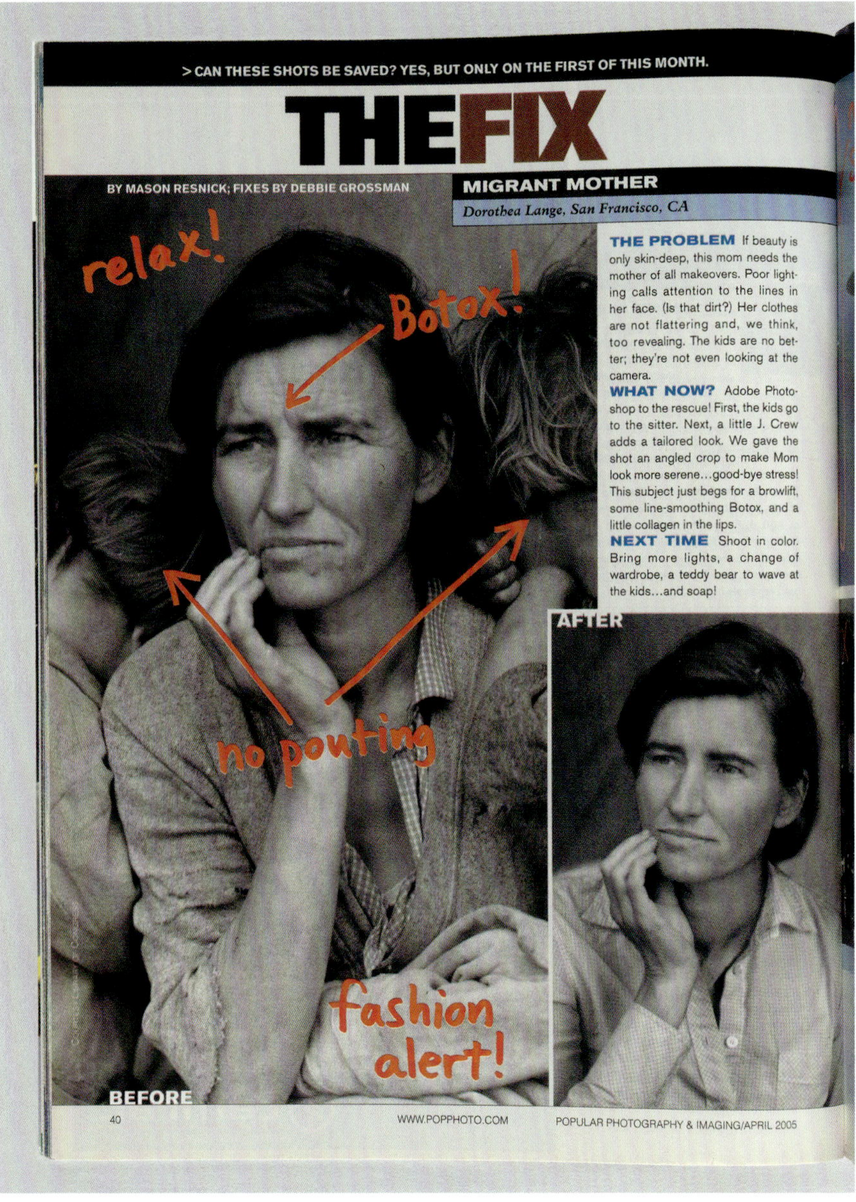

> CAN THESE SHOTS BE SAVED? YES, BUT ONLY ON THE FIRST OF THIS MONTH.

THE FIX

BY MASON RESNICK; FIXES BY DEBBIE GROSSMAN

MIGRANT MOTHER

Dorothea Lange, San Francisco, CA

THE PROBLEM If beauty is only skin-deep, this mom needs the mother of all makeovers. Poor lighting calls attention to the lines in her face. (Is that dirt?) Her clothes are not flattering and, we think, too revealing. The kids are no better; they're not even looking at the camera.

WHAT NOW? Adobe Photoshop to the rescue! First, the kids go to the sitter. Next, a little J. Crew adds a tailored look. We gave the shot an angled crop to make Mom look more serene...good-bye stress! This subject just begs for a browlift, some line-smoothing Botox, and a little collagen in the lips.

NEXT TIME Shoot in color. Bring more lights, a change of wardrobe, a teddy bear to wave at the kids...and soap!

relax!

Botox!

no pouting

fashion alert!

BEFORE

AFTER

40 WWW.POPPHOTO.COM POPULAR PHOTOGRAPHY & IMAGING/APRIL 2005

FIG. 29. "The Fix," by Mason Resnick, in *Popular Photography* 69, no. 4 (April 2005), p. 40. "Fixes" by Debbie Grossman. PHOTOGRAPHY DEPARTMENTAL COLLECTION, THE MUSEUM OF MODERN ART, NEW YORK. PURCHASE, 2018

the kids go to the sitter"), and added a few of their own tongue-in-cheek fixes ("Next, a little J. Crew adds a tailored look"). In a follow-up article, they revealed: "We received hundreds—yes, HUNDREDS—of rants, hate letters, and excommunication threats. Our wanton destruction of Dorothea Lange's 'Migrant Mother' generated particularly venomous indignation."[43] This instinct to protect *Migrant Mother* in its original form might be considered an expression of

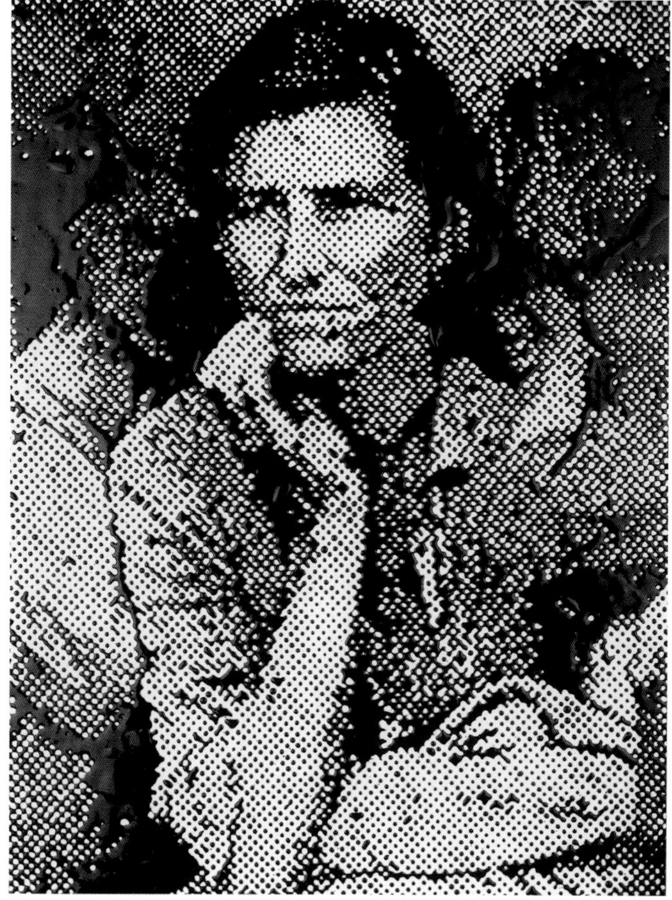

FIG. 30. Vik Muniz (Brazilian, b. 1961). *Migrant Mother, after Dorothea Lange.* 2000. Chromogenic color print (printed 2009), 39 9/16 x 29 5/8" (100.5 x 75.3 cm). THE MUSEUM OF MODERN ART, NEW YORK. LATIN AMERICAN AND CARIBBEAN FUND, 2009

Lange's personal credo, encapsulated in a quote from Francis Bacon that hung prominently in her studio from 1934 to the end of her life: "The contemplation of things as they are, without substitution or imposture, without error or confusion, is in itself a nobler thing than a whole harvest of invention."

Three-quarters of a century has passed since Lange met Florence Owens Thompson and her children in Nipomo, California. But far from receding into history, this image of a concerned mother with her hungry children has transcended the original circumstance of its creation and found a place in our common cultural consciousness. The artist Vik Muniz alludes to its mass circulation in his version of the image, rendered with drops of glistening ink evoking the half-tone screen of newspaper reproductions **[FIG. 30]**. We recognize Lange's photograph even when it has been reconstituted as a color painting in

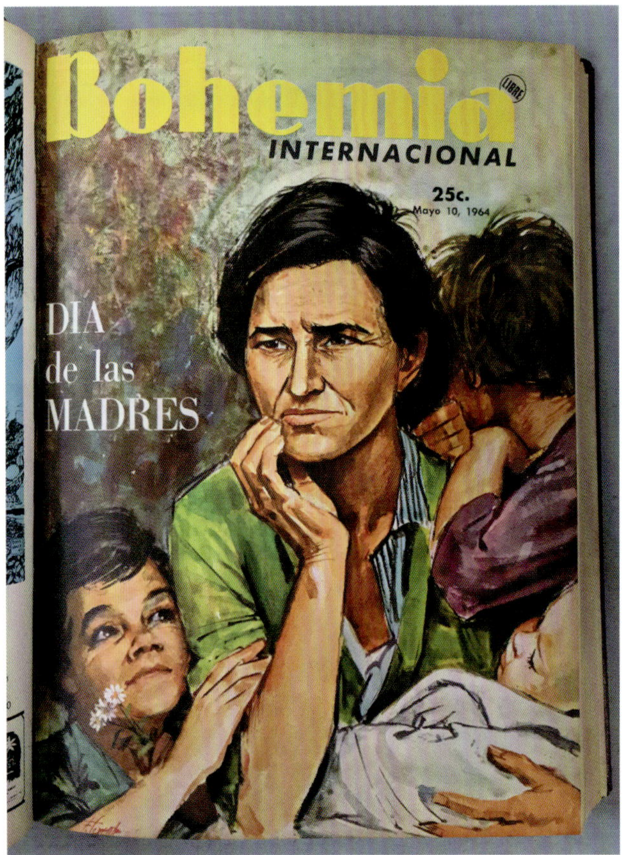

FIG. 31. "Día de las Madres." Cover of *Bohemia Internacional (Libre)* 55, no. 58 (May 10, 1964). Illustration by F. Lorente

which one child is turned toward the viewer, in a pencil drawing where the protagonists are African American, or when the central figure appears as a Walmart employee **[FIGS. 31, 32, 33]**. In 1978 Szarkowski mused:

> One could do very interesting research about all of the ways that the Migrant Mother has been used; all of the ways that it has been doctored, painted over, made to look Spanish and Russian; and all the things it has been used to prove. . . . Certainly one of the terribly interesting things about pictures is that they do attract to themselves wonderful rich bodies of speculation and superstition and fairy tale that, for better or worse, are part of what we're going to do to things that interest us.[44]

—

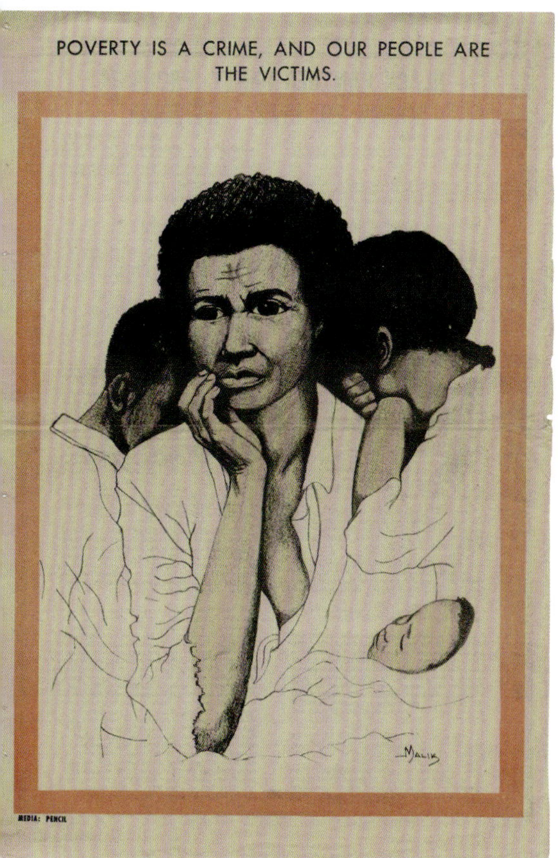

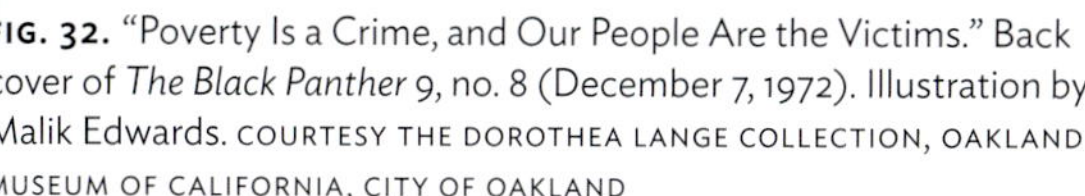
FIG. 32. "Poverty Is a Crime, and Our People Are the Victims." Back cover of *The Black Panther* 9, no. 8 (December 7, 1972). Illustration by Malik Edwards. COURTESY THE DOROTHEA LANGE COLLECTION, OAKLAND MUSEUM OF CALIFORNIA, CITY OF OAKLAND

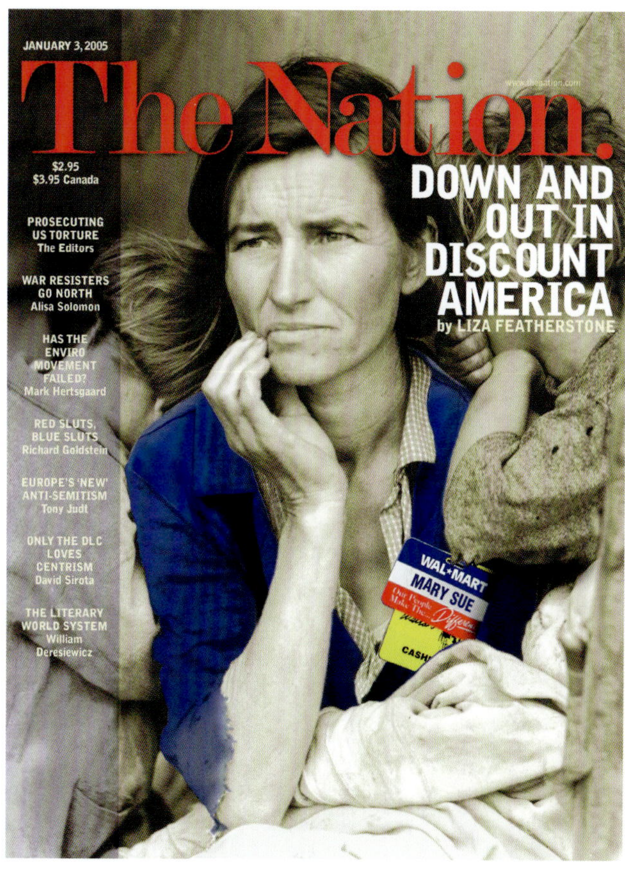

FIG. 33. "Down and Out in Discount America." Cover of *The Nation* 280, no. 1 (January 3, 2005). Illustration by Stephen Kling

Just as this photograph has been reproduced in countless formats and contexts and subjected to gross manipulation and tender tribute, it has also been the focus of much public discussion. Nevertheless it has spent a great deal of its life surrounded by myth—not without the help of Lange herself, whose recollections of that day in Nipomo were colored and reshaped over time, as memories often are. Lange's account of the creation of *Migrant Mother*, in what she described as "The Assignment I'll Never Forget," was published in *Popular Photography* in 1960 **[FIG. 34]**.[45] That she chose to refer to it as an "assignment" in this context downplays the role of her intuition and initiative in this consequential encounter. Before giving Lange the final word, let us consider the

No. 2

THE ASSIGNMENT I'LL NEVER FORGET

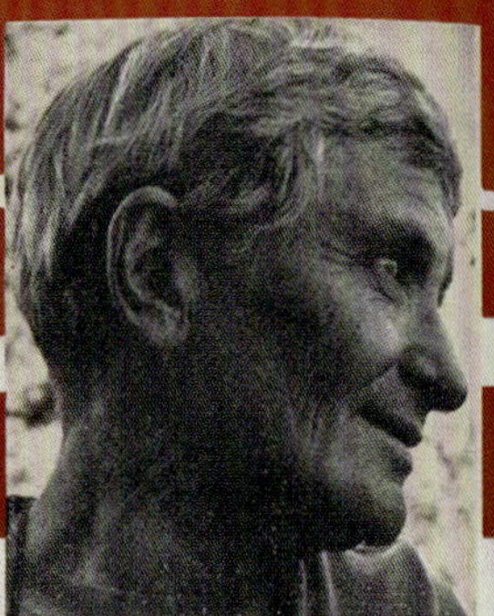

By DOROTHEA LANGE

MIGRANT MOTHER

A famed photojournalist tells of the picture that symbolized an era

When I began thinking of my most memorable assignments, instantly there flashed to mind the experience surrounding "Migrant Mother," an experience so vivid and well-remembered that I will attempt to pass it on to you.

As you look at the photograph of the migrant mother, you may well say to yourself: "How many times have I seen this one?" It is used and published over and over, all around the world, year after year, somewhat to my embarrassment for I am not a "one-picture photographer."

Once when I was complaining of the continual use and re-use of this photograph to the neglect of others I have produced in the course of a long career, an astute friend reproved me. "Time is the greatest of editors," he said, "and the most reliable. When a photograph stands this test, recognize and celebrate it."

Here then is that same picture, once again, and this time with the story. I have never captioned it other than with date and place. The circumstances surrounding it are not spectacular, but important to me in a different way.

"Migrant Mother" was made 23 years ago, in March, 1936, when I was on the team of Farm Security Administration photographers (called "Resettlement Administration" in the early days). Their duties and the scope of their work is a story well known to students of contemporary photography. We had a unique job, and the results of our travels over the U.S.A. have proved of real value.

(A "detour": to add that it is now high time, and the right time, to enable another band of perceptive cameramen to photograph our country, under intelligent guidance and auspices, if for no other reason than "just for the record." Just for the record, and the results of this recording to be gathered, annotated, distributed, and preserved for the future, in a central archive. "End of detour.")

To repeat, it was 23 years ago at the end of a cold, miserable winter. I had been traveling in the field alone for a month, photographing the migratory farm labor of California—the ways of life and the conditions of these people who serve and produce our great crops. My work was done, time was up, and I was worked out.

It was raining, the camera bags were packed, and I had on the seat beside me in the car the results of my long trip, the box containing all those rolls and packs of exposed film ready to mail back to Washington. It was a time of relief. Sixty-five miles an hour for seven hours would get me home to my family that night, and my eyes were glued to the wet and gleaming highway that stretched out ahead. I felt freed, for I could lift my mind off my job and think of home.

I WAS ON MY WAY and barely saw a crude sign with pointing arrow which flashed by at the side of the road, saying PEA-PICKERS CAMP. But out of the corner of my eye I *did* see it.

I didn't want to stop, and didn't. I didn't want to remember that I had seen it, so I drove on and ignored the summons. Then, accompanied by the rhythmic hum of the windshield wipers, arose an inner argument:

Dorothea, how about that camp back there?

What is the situation back there?

Are you going back?

Nobody could ask this of you, now could they?

To turn back certainly is not necessary. Haven't you plenty of negatives already on this subject? Isn't this just one more of the same? Besides, if you take a camera out in this rain, you're just asking for trouble. Now be reasonable, etc., etc., etc.

Having well convinced myself for 20 miles that I could continue on, I did the opposite. Almost without realizing what I was doing, I made a U-turn on the empty highway. I went back those 20 miles and turned off the highway at that sign, PEA-PICKERS CAMP.

continued on page 128

Dorothea Lange's "Migrant Mother" is one of the truly great American photographs, and her account of how the picture came to be taken is one of the finest and most moving articles POPULAR PHOTOGRAPHY has been privileged to publish.—*Bruce Downes*

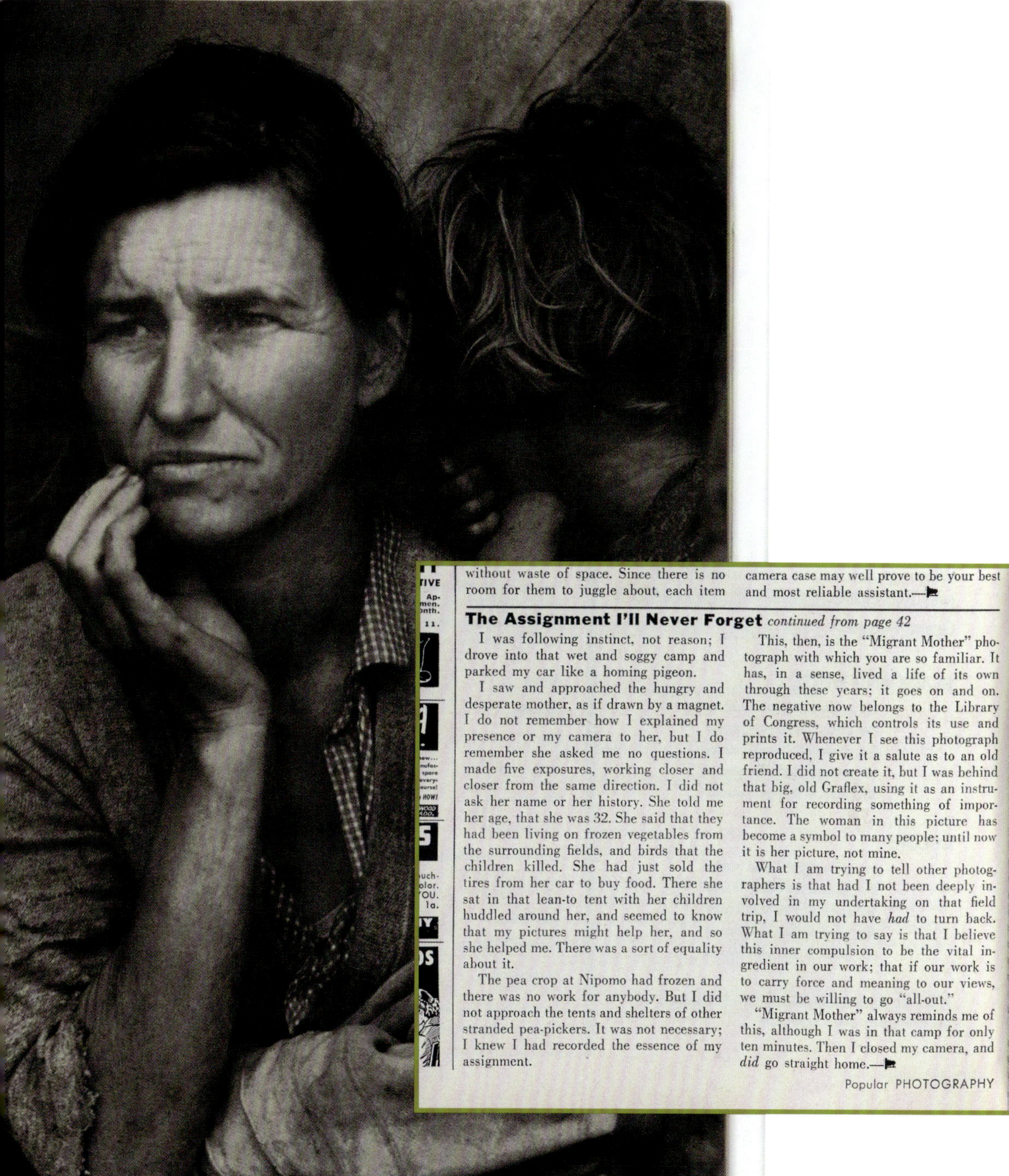

without waste of space. Since there is no room for them to juggle about, each item camera case may well prove to be your best and most reliable assistant.—

The Assignment I'll Never Forget *continued from page 42*

I was following instinct, not reason; I drove into that wet and soggy camp and parked my car like a homing pigeon.

I saw and approached the hungry and desperate mother, as if drawn by a magnet. I do not remember how I explained my presence or my camera to her, but I do remember she asked me no questions. I made five exposures, working closer and closer from the same direction. I did not ask her name or her history. She told me her age, that she was 32. She said that they had been living on frozen vegetables from the surrounding fields, and birds that the children killed. She had just sold the tires from her car to buy food. There she sat in that lean-to tent with her children huddled around her, and seemed to know that my pictures might help her, and so she helped me. There was a sort of equality about it.

The pea crop at Nipomo had frozen and there was no work for anybody. But I did not approach the tents and shelters of other stranded pea-pickers. It was not necessary; I knew I had recorded the essence of my assignment.

This, then, is the "Migrant Mother" photograph with which you are so familiar. It has, in a sense, lived a life of its own through these years; it goes on and on. The negative now belongs to the Library of Congress, which controls its use and prints it. Whenever I see this photograph reproduced, I give it a salute as to an old friend. I did not create it, but I was behind that big, old Graflex, using it as an instrument for recording something of importance. The woman in this picture has become a symbol to many people; until now it is her picture, not mine.

What I am trying to tell other photographers is that had I not been deeply involved in my undertaking on that field trip, I would not have *had* to turn back. What I am trying to say is that I believe this inner compulsion to be the vital ingredient in our work; that if our work is to carry force and meaning to our views, we must be willing to go "all-out."

"Migrant Mother" always reminds me of this, although I was in that camp for only ten minutes. Then I closed my camera, and *did* go straight home.—

selected as one of "50 Memorable Pictures of Last Half-Century" by a jury acting for University of Missouri.

FIG. 34. Dorothea Lange. "The Assignment I'll Never Forget." *Popular Photography* 46, no. 2 (June 1960), pp. 42–43, 126. PHOTOGRAPHY DEPARTMENTAL COLLECTION, THE MUSEUM OF MODERN ART, NEW YORK. PURCHASE, 2018

reflections of her dear friend and trusted printer Ansel Adams, who observed at the beginning of her career that Lange was

> an extraordinary phenomenon in photography. She is both a humanitarian and an artist. Her pictures of people show an uncanny perception, psychological and emotional, which is transmitted with immense impact on the spectator. To my mind, she presents the almost perfect balance between artist and human being. I am frankly critical of her technique in reference to the standards of purist photography, but I have nothing but admiration for the more important things—perception and intention. Her pictures are both records of actuality and exquisitely sensitive emotional documents. Her pictures tell you of many things; they tell you these things with conviction, directness, completeness. . . . If any documents of this turbulent age are justified to endure, the photographs of Dorothea Lange shall, most certainly.[46]

Although Lange rightfully resisted distilling her achievement to a single image, *Migrant Mother* has become central to our understanding of not only the history of photography but the history of the United States. It is a uniquely powerful example of the medium's ability to play multiple roles simultaneously: as a document of a moment, as a symbol of an era, and as a spur to the imagination across cultures and generations.

NOTES

1. Ed[win] Locke to Dorothea Lange, July 7, 1936. This and all subsequent correspondence between Lange and Stryker can be found in the Roy Stryker Papers, University of Louisville (Kentucky), and is accessible through the university's widely distributed microfilm edition. Kaitlin Booher provided invaluable research assistance throughout this project. I am deeply grateful for her contributions, as well as those of Drew Johnson at the Oakland Museum of California, and Sandra Phillips.

2. My thanks to Rob Slifkin and his student Damla Koksalan at the Institute of Fine Arts, New York University, for bringing this reference to my attention.

3. Any unattributed biographical details in this essay were drawn from Linda Gordon, *Dorothea Lange: A Life Beyond Limits* (New York: Norton, 2009). See also Milton Meltzer, *Dorothea Lange: A Photographer's Life* (New York: Farrar, Straus and Giroux, 1978).

4. Dorothea Lange, *The Making of a Documentary Photographer*, interview conducted in 1960–61 by Suzanne Riess (Berkeley: Regional Oral History Office, Bancroft Library, University of California, Berkeley, 1968), p. 17, available at www.lib.berkeley.edu/libraries/bancroft-library/oral-history-center.

5. In their engagement announcement in the *San Francisco Chronicle*, the paper referred to Lange as "a photographic artist of great talent, whose work has exceptional quality and feeling, and who has secured a large clientele since her arrival here a year and a half ago." *San Francisco Chronicle*, January 22, 1920, p. 3.

6. Lange, *The Making of a Documentary Photographer*, p. 92.

7. Ibid., p. 149.

8. George P. Elliott, "On Dorothea Lange," in John Szarkowski, ed., *Dorothea Lange* (New York: The Museum of Modern Art, 1966), p. 8.

9. Paul Schustçer Taylor, in Eugenia Parry Janis and Wendy MacNeil, eds., *Photography within the Humanities* (Danbury, N.H.: Addison House, 1977), p. 28. The article Taylor mentions was published in *Survey Graphic* 23, no. 9 (September 1934): 405–11.

10. This report, *Establishment of Rural Rehabilitation Camps for Migrants in California* (sometimes referred to as the Drobish report), is accessible digitally through the Library of Congress: https://lccn.loc.gov/2004678009.

11. See Sandra S. Phillips, "Dorothea Lange: An American Photographer," in *Dorothea Lange: American Photographs*, foreword by John R. Lane; essays by Therese Thau Heyman, Sandra S. Phillips, and John Szarkowski (San Francisco: Chronicle Books, in association with San Francisco Museum of Modern Art, 1994), p. 22.

12. Willard Van Dyke, "The Photographs of Dorothea Lange: A Critical Analysis," *Camera Craft* 41, no. 10 (October 1934): 462, 464.

13. Although the date on this card reads February 1936 (an understandable confusion as Lange had also visited Nipomo on February 21 and 22), through her correspondence with Stryker we can be certain the negatives were exposed after March 2, 1936, when she wrote: "Have two days work still to do in the Los Angeles area . . . then on to Santa Paula" (located in the direction of Nipomo along Highway 101). On February 24 she had outlined this plan: "I am expected in Los Angeles tomorrow night. The rains are about over. Had to get out of the San Luis [Obispo] area with the job unfinished before the road washed away. Will stop there again on the return trip."

14. Most descriptions of the circumstances surrounding the creation of this series of photographs are drawn from Lange's account as published in the June 1960 issue of *Popular Photography*; it is reproduced in its entirety on pp. 40–41 of this volume.

15. There are gaps and occasional inconsistencies in the surviving records. Lange's detailed handwritten notes for Lots 344 and 345 (corresponding to her travel in February and March 1936) include no reference to *Migrant Mother* (which makes sense if she was indeed rushing home). She wrote to Stryker on March 2, 1936: "I try to keep track of my exposures, but in a full and varied day there are lapses, and I know that I have missed out on some of my notes. [Here Lange pastes in a "Proverb of China": *The palest ink is better than the most retentive memory*.] Even so, sometimes it hasn't been possible, and some of the notations I shall have to make after I have the prints." The earliest typed captions with the RA/FSA are likely her response

to subsequent requests for information. On April 18, 1936, Stryker wrote to Lange: "You have sent in some swell stuff. We are very much pleased with it. We shall need captions for some of the prints." Heartfelt thanks to Micah Messenheimer, Beverly W. Brannan, and their colleagues at the Library of Congress for their support with this research.

16. Thompson's family has published a book that captures—through imaginative reconstructed dialogue—the story of her life. See Oleta Kay Sprague Ham and Roger Sprague, Sr., *Migrant Mother: The Untold Story, A Family Memoir* (Mustang, Okla.: Tate, 2013).

17. Lange, in *Popular Photography* (June 1960); see p. 41 of the present volume.

18. As noted in several of the captions (worded here verbatim as on the original file cards), Thompson was a thirty-two-year-old mother of seven children. Viola was her second-born. Three children were not at the camp when Lange visited: a daughter, Violet (fourteen), and two sons, Leroy (eleven) and Troy (nine). An eighth child (born in 1933) was sickly and may have died before 1936, which could explain why he wasn't mentioned. Ruby (six) wears a knit hat with a pompom in two images, and Katherine (four) wears a patterned dress beneath her jacket. These children's father, Cleo Owens, had passed away when Thompson was pregnant with Katherine. James Hill was the father of Norma, the baby in these photographs; Hill is the "native Californian" mentioned in the FSA captions.

19. These images contradict some details found in the most comprehensive of the captions from the RA/FSA files, which were likely derived (by Lange or an RA/FSA staff member) from United Press reports published in the *San Francisco News* and elsewhere (see figs. 15, 16, 17). Gregory Hom and Christina Moretta from the San Francisco Public Library were instrumental in obtaining this information.

20. Lange acknowledged five images from the series (the five currently located at the Library of Congress). A sixth [fig. 9] has regularly appeared in discussions of the series. The seventh image [fig. 12] was discovered in the late 1990s by art historian Sally Stein in the Oakland Museum files.

21. Roy Emerson Stryker and Nancy Wood, *In This Proud Land: America 1935–1943 as Seen in the FSA Photographs* (Greenwich, Conn.: New York Graphic Society, 1973), p. 19.

22. John Szarkowski, "Dorothea Lange and Paul Taylor," in *Dorothea Lange: American Photographs*, p. 49.

23. Lange, quoted in Gordon, *Dorothea Lange*, p. 110.

24. See Wendy Kozol, "Madonnas of the Fields: Photography, Gender, and 1930s Farm Relief," *Genders*, no. 2 (Summer 1988): 1–23.

25. On the subject of influence, Swensen wrote: "Even though Steinbeck never acknowledged Lange as his primary influence, many scholars concur that it was she who had the greatest visual impact on the author. . . . Steinbeck credited Lange's pictures as inspiring him to investigate the migrants' plight." James R. Swensen, *Picturing Migrants: The Grapes of Wrath and New Deal Documentary Photography* (Norman: University of Oklahoma Press, 2015), p. 39.

26. Emmett Corrigan, a reporter for the *Modesto Bee*, is credited with locating and interviewing Thompson in 1978, and it is likely he authored the article that circulated via the Associated Press. See for example "'Migrant Mother' Feels Exploited," *Los Angeles Times*, November 18, 1978. Clearly without understanding that neither Lange nor anyone else profited from the distribution of any FSA photographs, Thompson argued: "I can't get a penny out of it. [Lange] didn't ask my name. She said she wouldn't sell the pictures. She said she'd send me a copy. She never did." Linda Gordon reproduces the text from an earlier letter of complaint Thompson sent to *U.S. Camera* in 1958, although this letter never became public (Gordon, *Dorothea Lange*, p. 241).

27. See for example Jack Foley, "'Migrant Mother' Now Lies Dying: Subject of Photo Racked by Cancer," *San Jose Mercury News*, August 21, 1983; and "An Appeal for a Face from the Depression," *New York Times*, August 24, 1983. Despite this support, Thompson passed away on September 16, 1983.

28. For subsequent investigations, see Bill Ganzel, *Dust Bowl Descent* (Lincoln: University of Nebraska Press, 1984); and Geoffrey Dunn, "Photographic License," *San Jose Metro* 10, no. 27 (January 19–25, 1995). See http://archive.newtimesslo.com/archive/2003-10-22/archives/cov_stories_2002/cov_01172002.html (accessed April 8, 2018).

29. Sally Stein, "Passing Likeness: Dorothea Lange's 'Migrant Mother' and the Paradox of

Iconicity," in Coco Fusco and Brian Wallis, eds., *Only Skin Deep: Changing Visions of the American Self* (New York: International Center of Photography, in association with Abrams, 2003), p. 355.

30. Frank Crowninshield, "Forward," *U.S. Camera Annual 1939*, p. 11A.

31. The Library of Congress holds a bound album of fifty FSA photographs circulated by MoMA from the First International Photographic Exposition; http://www.loc.gov/pictures/item/2004677998/.

32. *Migrant Mother* was included in MoMA's exhibitions *Art in Progress* (1944, with the title "In a Camp of Migratory Pea Pickers, San Luis Obispo Co., Cal."); *The Museum Collection of Photographs* (1945); *Six Women Photographers: Photographs by Margaret Bourke-White, Helen Levitt, Dorothea Lange, Tana Hoban, Esther Bubley, and Hazel-Frieda Larsen* (1949; a new print, larger than the one Bender had given); and *Then and Now* (1952).

33. The Museum of Modern Art Exhibition Records, 516.3. The Museum of Modern Art Archives, New York.

34. See Lange to Stryker, May 16, 1939.

35. Press release for *The Family of Man*, issued January 26, 1955 (available online through www.moma.org). The record-breaking exhibition at MoMA closed May 8, 1955, and then toured nationally. The United States Information Agency subsequently circulated five versions of the exhibition across six continents; by the time the tour ended in 1965 an estimated 9.5 million people had seen it.

36. John Szarkowski wrote eloquently about Lange's contributions to *The Family of Man* in his essay "The Family of Man," in John Elderfield, ed., *The Museum of Modern Art at Mid-Century: At Home and Abroad*, Studies in Modern Art 4 (New York: The Museum of Modern Art, 1994), pp. 12–37.

37. In all, there were 203 photographs in *The Bitter Years*, which was on view from October 18 to November 25, 1962. Of the twenty-five reproductions in the accompanying catalogue, eight were photographs by Lange (no other photographer had more than three).

38. Press release for *Five Unrelated Photographers*, issued March 28, 1963 (exhibition dates, May 29–July 21, 1963; available at www.moma.org). Emphasis in original.

39. John Szarkowski to Dorothea Lange, February 28, 1964. Department of Photography correspondence files, The Museum of Modern Art, New York.

40. This topic is thoughtfully addressed in Mia Fineman, *Faking It: Manipulated Photography before Photoshop* (New York: Metropolitan Museum of Art, 2012).

41. Lange to Stryker, May 16, 1939.

42. This print was not further retouched for the August 30 reproduction, although it was reused on at least six occasions between 1966 and 1995.

43. Mason Resnick, "I can't believe you guys would stoop so low!" *Popular Photography*, December 16, 2008; www.popphoto.com/how-to/2008/12/i-cant-believe-you-guys-would-stoop-so-low (accessed May 8, 2018).

44. John Szarkowski, in Janis and MacNeil, eds., *Photography within the Humanities*, p. 95.

45. Careful readers will notice a few comments by Lange that have been disproved elsewhere in this text, and a few others that might be considered imperfect but well-intentioned recollections.

46. Ansel Adams, unpublished statement on Group f/64 (1934?), quoted in Nancy Newhall, *Ansel Adams: The Eloquent Light* (San Francisco: Sierra Club, 1963), p. 82.

FOR FURTHER READING

Curtis, James. "'The Contemplation of Things as They Are': Dorothea Lange and *Migrant Mother*." In *Mind's Eye, Mind's Truth: FSA Photography Reconsidered*. Philadelphia: Temple University Press, 1991.

Dorothea Lange: American Photographs. Foreword by John R. Lane. Essays by Therese Thau Heyman, Sandra S. Phillips, and John Szarkowski. San Francisco: Chronicle Books, in association with San Francisco Museum of Modern Art, 1994.

Fleischhauer, Carl, Beverly W. Brannan, Lawrence W. Levine, and Alan Trachtenberg. *Documenting America, 1935–1943*. Berkeley: University of California Press, in association with the Library of Congress, 1988.

Gordon, Linda. *Dorothea Lange: A Life Beyond Limits*. London: Norton, 2009.

Lange, Dorothea, and Paul Taylor. *An American Exodus: A Record of Human Erosion*. New York: Reynal & Hitchcock, 1939.

Meltzer, Milton. *Dorothea Lange: A Photographer's Life*. New York: Farrar, Straus and Giroux, 1978.

Partridge, Elizabeth, ed. *Dorothea Lange: A Visual Life*. Washington, D.C.: Smithsonian Institution Press, 1994.

Stein, Sally. "Passing Likeness: Dorothea Lange's 'Migrant Mother' and the Paradox of Iconicity." In Coco Fusco and Brian Wallis, eds., *Only Skin Deep: Changing Visions of the American Self*. New York: International Center of Photography, in association with Abrams, 2003.

Swensen, James R. *Picturing Migrants: The Grapes of Wrath and New Deal Documentary Photography*. Norman: University of Oklahoma Press, 2015.

Szarkowski, John, ed. *Dorothea Lange*. Introductory essay by George P. Elliott. New York: The Museum of Modern Art, 1966.

ALSO OF INTEREST

Photogrammar (website). Created and maintained by Laura Wexler et al. Yale University, New Haven, Conn. http://photogrammar.yale.edu/. (Accessed May 10, 2018.)

Taylor, Dyanna. "Dorothea Lange: Grab a Hunk of Lightning." From the *American Masters* television series. Aired August 29, 2014, on PBS. http://grabahunkoflightning.com/. (Accessed May 10, 2018.)

Produced by The Department of Publications
The Museum of Modern Art, New York

This publication was made possible by The Modern Women's Fund.

Edited by Diana C. Stoll
Designed by Miko McGinty and Rita Jules
Production by Matthew Pimm
Printed and bound by Ofset Yapimevi, Turkey

Typeset in Ideal Sans
Printed on 150 gsm Magno Satin

Second printing 2024

Library of Congress Control Number: 2018945655

ISBN: 978-1-63345-066-0

Published by The Museum of Modern Art
11 West 53 Street
New York, New York 10019-5497
www.moma.org

Distributed in the United States and Canada by ARTBOOK/D.A.P.
75 Broad Street, Suite 630, New York, New York 10004
www.artbook.com

Distributed outside the United States and Canada by Thames & Hudson Ltd.
181A High Holborn, London WC1V 7QX
www.thamesandhudson.com

Printed and bound in Turkey

PHOTOGRAPH CREDITS

In reproducing the images contained in this publication, the Museum obtained the permission of the rights holders whenever possible. If the Museum could not locate the rights holders, notwithstanding good-faith efforts, it requests that any contact information concerning such rights holders be forwarded so that they may be contacted for future editions.

© 2018 Bonnier Corporation; Department of Imaging and Visual Resources, The Museum of Modern Art, New York, photos by John Wronn: figs. 29, 34. Courtesy the Herb Caen Magazines and Newspaper Center of the San Francisco Public Library: figs. 15, 16, 17. © 2018 Estate of Imogen Cunningham; Department of Imaging and Visual Resources, The Museum of Modern Art, New York, photo by John Wronn: fig. 3. Farm Security Administration–Office of War Information Photograph Collection, Library of Congress: fig. 6 (LOC # LC-DIG-ppmsca-19155); fig. 7 (LOC # LC-USF34-002392-E); fig. 8 (LOC # LC-USF34-009058-C); fig. 10 (LOC # LC-USF34-009098-C); fig. 11 (LOC # LC-USF34-009097-C); fig. 13 (LOC # LC-USF34-009095-C); fig. 14 (LOC # LCUSF34-009093-C); fig. 19 (LOC # LC-USF34-000825-C); fig. 24 (LOC # LC-USF34- 026344-D). Digital Images © 2018 Department of Imaging and Visual Resources, The Museum of Modern Art, New York: figs. 18, 26; photo by Thomas Griesel: cover, inside back cover foldout; photos by John Wronn: figs. 1, 20, 22, 23, 28. © 2018 The Dorothea Lange Collection, Oakland Museum of California; Department of Imaging and Visual Resources, The Museum of Modern Art, New York: fig. 5; photo by John Wronn: fig. 4. © 2018 Vik Muniz/Licensed by VAGA, New York; Department of Imaging and Visual Resources, The Museum of Modern Art, New York, photo by John Wronn: fig. 30. © 2018 *The Nation*: fig. 33. © 1936 *The New York Times*: fig. 27. © 2018 Estate of Homer Page; The Museum of Modern Art Archives, New York, Edward Steichen Archive, V.B.i.8; Department of Imaging and Visual Resources, The Museum of Modern Art, New York, photo by John Wronn: fig. 25. © 2018 Warner Brothers: fig. 2.

TRUSTEES OF THE MUSEUM OF MODERN ART